MW00834447

WILD
THING

A Rocky Road

Pete Staples

NEW HAVEN PUBLISHING LTD

WILD THING

First Edition
Published 2017
NEW HAVEN PUBLISHING LTD
www.newhavenpublishingltd.com
newhavenpublishing@gmail.com

Front Cover Photo©Rex by Shutterstock
Back cover Photos©Courtesy of the Author
Cover design©Pete Cunliffe
pcunliffe@blueyonder.co.uk

newhaven
publishing

INTRODUCTION

"Cor, you could write a book Pete," they would say, after I told them stories about my youth and the pop groups I've played in. This I found very amusing, and I always laughed it off, until an American writer contacted me and said he would like to do my autobiography. Then I thought, perhaps there might be some interest in my very diverse life. Perhaps I could tell them about the day I took a shark for a ride on my pushbike; the things we got up to when we were semipro travelling around in an old van; having a worldwide hit with 'Wild Thing' and how it changed our lives; how I was betrayed by my friends, the dodgy managers, contracts and the loss of hundreds of thousands of pounds of record royalties; the heartache I felt after losing our first child, but the blessing of having a wonderful wife and children. Yes! I think I could do that, maybe better than anybody else. So, from the day I was born, my nursery, my school days, working in a butcher's shop, being an electrician, pop star, antique dealer, woodwork factory owner and trainee pub manager until the present day, it's all in this book.

After reading a few pop autobiographies, I found some of them so serious and up their own arses that I knew mine would have to be a lot more fun, but with a serious side to it as well. I hope it will make you laugh, gasp and maybe shed a little tear, but most of all enjoy it, just as I've enjoyed reliving it.

Pete Staples

CHAPTER 1

I was born on 3rd May 1944 Peter Lawrence Staples at Bachelors Barn Road, Andover, Hants. For those of you who have never heard of Andover it is a small market town in Hampshire not far from Salisbury and Winchester. In the 40s it had a population of about 11,000 and there were two major employers, Kelly's Directories and Taskers. Taskers were famous for making the Queen Mary; no, not the ship, but a transporter vehicle for the RAF in the war. If you didn't work at Kelly's or Taskers the only other work available would be in shops, building sites or farm work.

I was the youngest son of Percy and Violet Staples and had an older brother Gerald and sister Shirley. Mum also had another child before she married Dad, named Keith, and I will talk more about Keith later. Like everyone else I don't remember anything about my very early days, only what other people have remembered. I was told that when I was very young I had pneumonia and I'm convinced that my mother would have been very worried, as this was a killer then. When growing up she would always be rubbing camphorated oil on my chest, even in my teens; when going to the doctors, no matter what my problem was, she would always say "Get him to check your chest." Can you imagine going to the doctors with haemorrhoids or something just as intimate and asking "Can you also listen to my chest"? I also found out that for the first few months of my life my cot was the bottom drawer of the chest of drawers in Mum and Dad's bedroom. This might sound strange and a bit primitive to people these days, but this was not unusual then as it was warm, free from draughts, did the job and didn't cost anything.

WILD THING

My first memories were at the nursery in New Street, which was purpose built at the end of the war for children whose parents had to work to supplement their meagre war rations; this would be the case for most families. My mum worked in the kitchen at New Street School, which Gerald and Shirley attended, just over the road from my nursery. She would drop me at the nursery before going to work then pick me up in the afternoon. As I mentioned, the nursery was built just after the war and was prefabricated, consisting of a large hall, office, cloakroom, toilets, kitchen and a changing area. It was approximately 20m long and 5m wide and the hall acted as a play/dining area in the morning and a sleeping area in the afternoon. What I most remember about my nursery days was being made to have a sleep in the afternoons. At the end of the hall there was a big stack of tiny beds that looked more like boxes, and in the afternoons these would be placed in two rows the full length of the hall with a small mattress and blanket placed in each one, the idea being that we would fall asleep in them. I didn't mind going in the boxes, as I was quite used to sleeping in a drawer when I was born; perhaps that's why I've got claustrophobia. But I did find it difficult sleeping and quite often just lay there waiting for the staff to come around to wake us up ready for our mums to pick us up. I would stand at the window just waiting for Mum to arrive. Even now I can feel the joy I felt when I saw her coming through the gate to take me home.

Nursery photograph 1947. I'm 2nd row 4th from the right. What a poor looking bunch

5

1946 Shirley, Gerald and I

The land that the nursery was built on was where Etwall House originally stood and the hall in the nursery was where my musical career started many years later.

As this area of the town was so pivotal to my early and teenage years I've included a little local history and added an article from the Andover Advertiser. This was a report on the fire at Etwall House at which broke out at midnight on 11th May 1935 and led to its ultimate demise.

Etwall House, a large three-storey building fronts the New Street entrance to the Parish church, a fence separating the front garden from the churchyard path. It was built towards the end of the 18ᵗʰ century, before the abolition of the window tax 1851 and the site facing New Street presents bricked in window outlines. Mr Rule a director of the Satisfaction Company limited, who lived alone in the flat. Police sergeant Hudd and police Constable Newman were on duty in the High Street when they noticed smoke blowing from the north east. Proceeding to investigate they were met by a motorist who informed them that the upper part of Etwall House was ablaze and then went on to call the fire brigade. PS Hudd and PC Newman rushed to the burning building. The heavy front door resisted their onslaught, as did also the drive gate, but they were able to enter the garden at the rear of the building by the side door. After an unsuccessful attempt to enter the building by breaking the window they burst open the back door and started to tour the house to see if anyone was inside. All doors were locked and they had to burst them open. Arriving at the second floor where the fire was raging, they burst open the door of the bedroom occupied by Mr Rule. The blazing rafters were falling as they did so. Satisfied no one could be alive in such an inferno the police retraced their steps and were met on the ground floor by the Vicar of Andover, the Rev P F Morell, who had some knowledge of the house and with him they commenced a second tour, but could only reach the first floor because the heat and falling beams. There was no response to their shouts and knocking, which had aroused residence in New Street a 100 yards away. In the meantime, the fire brigade and captain FA Beale arrived and were directing three jets on the building from the yard of the premises adjoining the church. Some minutes after the arrival of the brigade and while the police and the vicar was still inside the blazing building, the crowd attracted to the scene, were amazed and horrified to see the figure of a man at the second floor window, silhouetted against the flames. The bottom section of the window resisted his efforts to open it, and he pulled down the upper part and hauled himself over, took one look round and then jumped falling into an ornamental flower bed on the front lawn. Firemen got him away from the heat and from the timber and the falling masonry. It was reported that as Mr Rule jumped and cries could be heard from his Aberdeen Terrier, Jock, who sadly perished. Across the courtyard were the stables but these were not affected by the fire.

New Street had quite a number of thatched houses, but fortunately they were at the other end of the street and were not near Etwall House. but they did not escape the dangers of fire as on Easter Monday 19th April, 1901 a fire broke out in a pub at the end of new Street and 17 cottages were destroyed and nearly a hundred people were made homeless.

Let us now move on from this sad period to my move to New Street Infant school.

CHAPTER 2

There are two things I remember most about my time at the infant school: the headmistress Miss Ethridge, and Marion, a girl I really liked. Miss Ethridge was a short stocky lady with a red face and a double chin. When she was using a very large megaphone in the playground and shouting out her orders to great effect, I would stand watching her, fascinated by her double chin flopping up and down. I thought that she looked like a pelican trying to swallow a big fish. It was at the infant school when I was seven that I tried to impress a little girl called Marion, who I very much wanted as my girlfriend. I was so keen for her to like me that, unbeknown to my parents, I took my grandfather's First World War naval medals from the drawer and gave them to her. These were the Pip, Squeak and Wilfred and were the World War One campaign medals. I don't think my grandfather saw a lot of action, but he did spend some time on the HMS Thunderer, a ship they called unlucky, because of two very serious accidents. The first was in 1876: whilst on full power trials out of Portsmouth, the boilers blew up killing the commanding officer and 45 others, also injuring a further 70.

The second mishap occurred when the 12.5 inch turret gun was double loaded, this time killing 11 and injuring a further 35. Fortunately, my grandfather was not on the ship during these accidents, but looking back and realising the significance of what I'd given away leaves me feeling somewhat embarrassed - but nowhere near as embarrassed as I felt having to ask for them back!

After infants, I moved to the primary school, which was on the same site but divided by a dark alleyway. At the end of the alley was a small playground and a brick outside toilet block, one half for the girls, the other for the boys. It was 25m from the classrooms. This location had both advantages and drawbacks. The drawback being, when it was very cold, you didn't hang around out there and just wanted to get back into the warmth of the main building as quickly as possible. This could encourage you to put your willie away before you had really finished, and in those days we only changed our white cotton pants on Fridays. (I will say no more on that.) The advantage of it being outside was that during the winter the pipes would get frozen, so we could not use the toilets and were sent home until it thawed. Sometimes it would be snowing, so this unexpected break from school was a marvellous time to get the sledges out and play.

After Christmas we were allowed to take one of our Christmas presents to school and show the class. Once a boy brought in a magic set and showed us a trick; this really fascinated me, capturing my imagination and starting my lifelong interest in that art. I was not academic and usually in the end of term exams I ended up in the lower 20s in a class of about 40. But I was good at sports and played in goal for the school, a position that I maintained in the Boys' Brigade and at the Senior School. Although I am mainly known for being in The Troggs my notoriety could have been quite different.

Every break time, our teacher Mr Rees would allocate the job of putting the kettle on in the teachers' rest room for their morning cuppa. One fateful day the job was given to me. I had to fill the kettle up with water, place it on the gas ring which was attached by a piece of rubber tube to the gas tap, and light the ring; then I could go out to play. This I did. Returning to the classroom after play Mr Rees called me over to his desk, pointed to the top of the desk and in his loud Welsh voice shouted "What do you think that is?" Staring at the pencils and pens and a piece of old rubber tube, I didn't know which one he was referring to, and looking at his wild eyes and big red face I thought my best bet was to say nothing. With no response from me, he curtly ordered me to follow him. I had no idea as to what on earth I had done as he briskly marched out of the classroom, with me trotting behind, and into the staff room. We were greeted by a very strong acrid smell of smoke and a thick grey haze that filled the room. It was then, in a very loud voice, he said that when he came to make the tea he'd found the room filled with smoke and then on frantic investigation discovered I had put the rubber gas tube too close to the burner and it was burning. The fright and shock of what I had done must have shown on my ten year old face as he then quietened down a bit. After telling me that I could have burnt the whole school down and how careless I was, we returned to the classroom and no more was ever said about it. I don't think any child in the class was ever asked to be a kettle monitor again; I know I wasn't. When I think of the fire at Etwall House and the seventeen properties destroyed by fire in New Street, I could have caused just as much havoc at my primary school and most likely I would not have been remembered as Pete from The Troggs but as the kid that burnt down New Street School.

The cold outside toilets at New St School

New Street Primary School after it closed in the late 60s

1948 Me at New Street Primary School and me in my school uniform – cap
and badge

From the age of eight until I left school at fifteen my leisure
time was taken up with the Life Boys followed by the Boys'

Brigade. The Life Boys were the junior leg of the Boys' Brigade and we met once a week for uniform inspection and games. Being a Christian organisation we had Bible class on Sunday and met at Etwall Hall; this was the old coach house of the demolished Etwall House, and it was taken over by the Boys' Brigade and refurbished to become their meeting place. In the early 50s the demand for a nursery seems to have declined and my nursery hall was handed over to Skipper Harris, the Captain of the 2nd Andover Boys' Brigade Company, for their new headquarters. This was done by Mr Moore, a local businessman and councillor, and the hall was named after him, so I will now refer to it as Moore Hall and not my nursery.

After failing the 11+ I attended Andover Boys' Secondary Modern School in London Road, which was a couple of hundred yards from where I lived. My brother Gerald was in his second year and my sister Shirley by then had left the girls' school opposite and was now working in The Milk Bar, a café in the High St.

Starting a new school was always a frightening experience, especially when they called it the 'big boys' school', where some of the boys could be fifteen years old. Fortunately, I had my brother there, who was quite a big chap and would stick up for me if I got into any bother; this was very welcome at the time but when I got home he would beat me up for getting into trouble, so I was no better off than any of the other boys.

As I said, I was not very academic, and that did not change when I went to the secondary school, but I did enjoy science, swimming and playing in goal for the school. There was one significant event that occurred there. Our school was playing Andover Grammar School at rugby. At the end of the match I saw this blonde quite handsome lad come staggering off the pitch with his shorts and shirt covered in grass stains, and blood. This young lad turned out to be Chris Britton who became our lead guitarist in The Troggs.

CHAPTER 3

As I mentioned, my interest in magic started when I was at the infant school with that boy who brought in his magic set after Christmas. I don't know if it was the magic or the attention he got that appealed to me, but it ignited my love of magic which has persisted to the present day.

When I was about eleven years old I started to do magic tricks at home in front of the mirror and bought many books about the subject. There was a book shop in Andover High Street called Clarks, and for me this shop was magic in itself. It was very old building and sold second-hand books; there was so many books that they were stacked from floor to ceiling and in search of my magic books I would need to walk down narrow passages that were illuminated by one 60W bulb hanging from a flex covered in cobwebs. It was such an exciting moment when I found a book I could afford, then dusted it off and just stood there in the half lit passage reading it.

Some of the materials for the tricks could be found at home, like handkerchiefs and Mum's satin scarves that I would mutilate to perform a trick. Some tricks could be purchased from a catalogue 'Ellisdon's of London'. The descriptions in Ellisdon's catalogues would today be a violation of the Trade Descriptions Act. Once, I thought it would be a good idea to be a ventriloquist, to add to my magic show, so I sent away for a booklet on 'How to be a ventriloquist'. With the book came a device you could put in your mouth to whistle like a bird. The book's entire instructions, in so many words, said, "To be a ventriloquist you must stand in front of the mirror and speak without moving your lips" (I wondered how they did it).

I can't really remember, but I think I must have paid for the tricks with the money I got from the paper round I did for Smith's. I earned 15 shillings a week which was quite a lot of money for a paper boy, but it was a very large round. Smith's supplied a bicycle, a very heavy machine with no gears and two panniers on the back. On many occasions they were completely full, making it very hard to pedal, especially when the monthly magazines were out. I remember one magazine I used to look forward to, called Health And Efficiency. This carried reviews and pictures of people in nudist camps. As censorship was very strict then, male genitalia was usually hidden under a table or behind table tennis bats, and the female fannies were rubbed out completely; this was a bit disappointing for a nosey young lad whose testosterone was on the rise (I think I could have phrased that a little better.) Anyhow back to magic. Some other tricks could be a little bit more dangerous; I'm not talking of Houdini dangerous, but that they contained chemicals. I remember doing a little show in Moore Hall for the BB and having to use hydrochloric acid and ammonia. When you add these two chemicals together they give off smoke, but before the curtains were opened the fumes from the two chemicals hidden on my table came in contact earlier than intended, and the first the audience saw of me was waving my hands frantically to dispel the smoke. I think I could have been the first Tommy Cooper. It's quite amazing to think in the late 50s a 13-year-old boy could go into a chemist and say "Could I have a bottle of hydrochloric acid and a bottle of ammonia please?" and be served.

Every Friday after BB I would run to my aunt Amy's house, just over the road from where we lived, to watch David Nixon's 'It's Magic' on their TV. At that particular time we didn't have a TV and it would take my father a couple of industrial accidents and the loss of half a finger and a big toe to have enough money, using the compensation payout to afford one.

One Friday BB had finished late and I thought I was going to miss 'It's Magic', so I ran as fast as I could to auntie Amy's, and knocked on the door waited until a voice called out, "Come in, you're late." I ran in and sat down just in time to see this magician pull doves from a handkerchief. Well, this really freaked me out and I knew I would have to get some doves. Unfortunately, I didn't know how or where.

My Uncle Sam was a caretaker at the Guildhall, and he was always talking about those "bloody pigeons" that he had to get out of the hall when the main doors were left open in the summer. So, with cage in hand I went to the Guildhall and asked him if I could have a couple of the pigeons. He had a very ingenious way of catching them. He would get a pillow and throw it at them as they sat in the roof space. They would be brought down with the pillow and it wasn't long before I had two pigeons in my cage and was on my way home.

I kept the cage in my bedroom so I could feed them and hoped they would get to know and trust me. But Mum moaned so much about the feathers and seed all over the place I was told I would have to keep them in the coal shed, out the back. Getting them to sit on my finger was an achievement, but trying to conceal them on me seemed an impossible task as they flapped their wings so much when I tried to push them inside my jacket pocket. I soon realised that I was not going to baffle anybody with my amazing birds as they seemed too big and uncooperative, so I decided to stay with the more basic tricks. I still kept the birds and they did become more friendly, and I could let them out their cage before I went to school in the morning and at 4 o'clock when I got home I would stand in the garden with a tin of corn, shake it and they would come down for their evening meal and then go back in their cage.

Mum said the neighbours were starting to complain about those "bloody pigeons" as they were shitting on their window sills. I didn't want to - or didn't know how to - get rid of them. However, fate took over one morning when I went down to let them out and found the cage door open and the two birds dead on the floor with big chunks out of their necks. I think the rats got them. I don't think Mum was too upset and the neighbours must have been pleased not having them shitting on their windows sills any more. In retrospect I think it would have been better to have left them at the Guildhall where they would have had only my Uncle Sam's pillow flooring them every so often.

CHAPTER 4

My first musical instrument was a ukulele that Dad bought for me when I was eight. He got it from the market as a Christmas present. I say present in the singular, because we usually only got one proper present, plus sweets, and an apple and an orange. All this was left at the bottom of our bed, in a pillowcase, on Christmas Eve. The ukulele came boxed with a picture of a hula hula girl on the front, and with complete instructions on how to form the chords of some simple songs. As we only had one or two toys, that's what you played with. There were no computers or computer games, in fact nothing electronic; most of the toys were push along or clockwork and, even today, I still think that they are more fascinating. Learning the chords and singing my first song ('Swanee River') gave me such a feeling of achievement that I carried on and learnt more tunes. (Could this have been the start of my rock 'n' roll career?). I often used to pick up my ukulele and start strumming and singing and Mum would look at me smile and remark, "That sounds nice." The attention I got, and pleasing other people, ticked all my boxes.

One day my brother Gerald was playing up, and Mum got so angry with him that she picked up the nearest thing to her and hit him over the head with it. Unfortunately, that thing was my ukulele; as he ran out of the room howling I stood there with my mouth open, not worried if he was hurt, but more concerned about the big piece of plastic that flew off my instrument. Fortunately, it was still playable and Gerald only had a bump on his head.

When I was young most streets had a family that would be forever trying to sell you things, most probably things they had got from jumble sales. One day I was approached by a young boy in my street saying he had an old guitar and would I like to buy it. I said I would like to see it first, so he went indoors and came out with this quite crude looking thing, which he handed to me. I played a chord, one that I would play on the ukulele, and it certainly had a fuller sound that I liked. I can't remember exactly how much it cost, or where I got the money from, but I did end up with it: my first guitar. I then needed to buy a book on guitar chords as the ukulele had four strings and the guitar six making the chord formation more complex. It was exasperating sometimes learning the chords, but once you mastered it it was such a marvellous feeling, strumming along with the latest songs being played on the radio.

Skiffle was just kicking off and there were quite a few young boys playing the guitar, albeit only about four chords which was all you really needed for skiffle. With a washboard and thimbles and a bass made out of a tea chest, broom handle and a piece of string, you had your skiffle group. We had our own little group in our road which was great fun, but with football, riding our bikes and making camps, it was just one of those passing crazes like Davy Crockett hats, bows and arrows and yo-yos. Soon everybody was doing their own separate things and not bothering with the guitars. It's not until I took my guitar to the BB once that I started to play and sing again with other people.

As I mentioned, from the age of eight until eleven I was in the Life Boys, then I joined the Boys' Brigade which used Etwall Hall and Moore Hall for their meetings and activities. Being in the BB I had some of the best times of my life, and it also opened the door to my career with pop groups. So much of my time was taken up with the BB. Once a week we met as a company for uniform inspection, marching, prayers and afterwards we had gym and team games. In the week you could do fencing, woodwork, band practice and football. As I loved music I decided I would like to join the band, but everybody seemed to want to be a drummer or a bugler and there were only vacancies for flute players, which didn't appeal to me one bit, so it was suggested that perhaps I would like to be a drum major, as this would make the band look more professional and add a bit more interest, with somebody being out front twisting the mace and throwing it in the air. This really appealed to me - giving orders and doing a bit of showing off - so I agreed. I don't know where it came from but they found an old mace; but of course, nobody knew what to do with it. Fortunately, one of the boys' fathers was in an RAF band and he offered to show me what to do. I was quite concerned when he told me my job as drum major was controlling the whole of the band, consisting of about 40 people of all ranks, from privates to officers, with me shouting my commands and them following the instructions.

Once I had learnt the instructions I then needed to learn how to do all the other fancy stuff. This was taught to me by an army drum major. I was amazed watching him spin the mace then twist it around his back then throw it in the air and catch it again; I thought yes! I could really do this and get a lot of the desired attention.

Because I was not allowed to take the mace home to practise - and I did need a lot of practice - I had to use my mother's broom. I spent many hours marching up and down the garden twisting, throwing and dropping the broom, putting the head back on and starting again. I don't know what the neighbours must have thought as they watched me, but I had to practise. The first time I got in front of the band I felt very nervous seeing all those faces looking and waiting for my commands; in retrospect it's like standing up in front of your class and reading something out for the first time, or your first gig in a band. I'm sure the band found it very helpful having somebody in front shouting out the commands and leading the way. Eventually I was given a sash and some white gloves; I think this was like saying "You've got the job". We had band practice every Friday and the first Sunday in the month was church parade; in the summer we did fetes and carnivals and we also did Remembrance Sunday parades. I enjoyed the marching with the band and the attention that I got.

'Boys' Brigade Church Parade. Me in my second hand suit

When we went to camp, the advance party would set up the tents and latrines prior to the company arriving. The band and company would march from the station to the camp site. This was usually quite an impressive show as we marched through villages and people would rush out of their cottages to watch as we marched by. I remember once marching down a lane to the camp and noticing the advance party ahead, standing in the middle of the lane with a gate either side. I didn't know which gate to go through, until one of the advance party waved to the right. With the mace outstretched I led the company through the gate, as the drums and bugles echoed around the surrounding hills. As we approached the tents they seemed to be a different style to what we normally used. Suddenly, girls came running out of the tents laughing and screaming... it was a Girl Guides camp and the advance party had played a joke and directed us through the wrong gate. The drums and bugles that were echoing around the hills suddenly started to dissipate. Being drum major I had to make a decision on what to do: should I keep marching or stop? With a bit of quick thinking I gave the command to counter march, which meant I had to march back down through

20

the ranks and they would follow. We made our impressive exit out of the field and back through the correct gate opposite.

The advance party had disappeared. I did however confront the officer about directing me through the wrong gate, and his excuse was that he didn't direct me, he was just brushing away a fly in front of his face. This embarrassing episode did however have a very pleasant outcome. Skipper Harris went over to apologise to the Guide mistress about our intrusion, and apparently she said there was nothing to apologise for, the girls really enjoyed it and found it very amusing, and furthermore, "Would your company like to come over one evening for cocoa and a sing along with us?" I remember the evening very well, the singing and the girls serving us with cocoa, but when it was time for us to return to our own camp Skipper and the officers had a very difficult job of trying to get us away from the girls and their hospitality.

As I mentioned, I was not academic but I did like sport and swam backstroke for my school and played in goal for the school and the BB. We had a very good six-a-side team in the BB and won a medal in Southampton District Six-a-side Tournament. I was very proud of my medal as not one ball passed over the goal line. This was not because I was a Peter Shilton but more due to the fact that my team were so good - I only touched the ball twice in the whole of the competition. I remember the occasion so well as it rained all day and the pitches were like quagmires. I did feel a bit embarrassed when I collected my medal as the other five looked like mudlarks and I had only two specks of mud on my pristine white shorts. I still meet up with some of my old BB friends for lunch, and love to watch their mouths drop open when I mention winning the medal and how I had to dive in the mud and stop the ball crossing the goal-line.

'Boys' Brigade 6 a side team back row: John Randall, David Stockwell and David Cox. Front row: Rodney White, me and Barry Grace

CHAPTER 5

Looking back we didn't have very much compared with what they have today. I think the bulk of my clothes were either hand-me-downs from Gerald or from a jumble sale. One of my favourite stories I like tell is that if I had a button missing from the collar of my shirt and Mum didn't have time to sew one on, she would get a needle and cotton and tie a knot where the button would normally be. The two ends left dangling were usually cut off with the carving knife just under my chin; this was bloody scary as Mum usually had a cigarette hanging out of her mouth, and with smoke going in her eyes making her squint she would hack away at the cotton. If she didn't have a carving knife handy she would take the cigarette out of her mouth grab hold of the two ends and I would watch in terror as the hot end of her cigarette disappeared under my chin to burn off the two ends, while she shouted "Keep still or you'll get burnt!" I can't tell you how frightened I was with my head tilted backwards looking up at the ceiling, clenching my fists in fear. But all in all our childhood was not too bad, especially when Dad got the compensation for losing a toe and finger when working for an engineering company. His lost his finger whilst drilling a steel band in the vice when it came out and whipped his index finger off. He lost a big toe when it got crushed after a steel girdle was dropped on it. Being so accident prone I sometimes wonder if his dad was on the 'Thunderer' when they double loaded the gun.

I remember the day the cheque arrived for one of the accidents. It was made out to cash and as Dad didn't have a cheque account, me and Mum went down to the bank on Saturday to cash it. Standing at the counter in the bank I held open a shopping bag as Mum scooped the £5 and £10 notes in with such gusto it must have looked to any bystander as if we were robbing the bank. My dad was in complete control of the finances of the house and after our trip to the bank I can see why. Between leaving the bank with our shopping bag stuffed with money and getting back home, my mum had called into Ponds the furniture shop and bought three beds and three mattresses for the whole family - this was a big chunk of the money gone.

The items were delivered in the afternoon and were stacked in the front room. When Dad got home in the evening from his weekly visit to the Walled Meadow watching Andover play football, he was confronted with a front room stacked full of new beds and mattresses. The atmosphere soon became very uncomfortable as he asked "Where the bloody hell did this this lot come from?" Mum tried to convince him that we all needed new beds and mattresses, but my dad was having none of it and all but one mattress was sent back. Out of his compensation Dad did buy the latest GEC TV complete with sliding door; this I thought was far better than any new bed or mattress.

CHAPTER 6

When it was time for me to leave school I had a few ideas of what I would like to do, either work for British Rail on the trains or be a policeman. While I was contemplating this, my mother decided that she would get me a job to 'tide me over.' Gerald was employed as an apprentice mechanic and Shirley worked in The Milk Bar Café; they were not very well paid so a little extra money would certainly help. The job she found for me was making sausages and faggots in a small prefabricated building at the back of Howard's, the butchers and fishmongers in the High Street. After a few lessons on mixing and using the machines from George, who then went out on the road delivering, I soon became a fully qualified sausage and faggot maker. I quite enjoyed it there, and could get cheap meat, sausages, faggots and fish. Working at Howard's had certain benefits and did help with our family budget. I also got on very well with Judy who worked there, and on Wednesdays, our half day, we would meet up and go out together. She was about three years older than me: I was 15 and she was about 18 and a lot more experienced in boy/girl relationships. (More about my seduction later).

When the BB decided to hold a dance we invited girls from Westholme, a local private girls school. I was asked by one of the boys' mothers if I could get some sausage meat so she could make some sausage rolls for the occasion. I was happy to do so, and at work the next day I made some extra; well, quite a lot really (the size of a small football). Pleased I could make this large contribution, I arrived at her house and knocked on the back door, and when she opened the door I smiled and said "I've got the meat." She invited me in and I dumped this big bag on the worktop.

When she saw the amount I had made her mouth dropped open, and she said "I can't make that many" and could I take some back? I couldn't take it back to the shop, so I had to take it home, and we had sausage meat fritters for days after that.

The preparation for the dance was nearly complete, apart from the drinks and how to keep them cool. We had a big chest freezer that didn't work, but we could still use it if we put ice in it. Again, I came to the rescue, mentioning that the fish department at Howard's used ice all the time and I could get several buckets of it, which I would put in the chest on my way home on the night of the dance. It was only about 400 yards from Howard's to Moore Hall, so I managed two trips and emptied the four buckets into the broken down fridge and closed the lid. I then went home, washed and changed into my glad-rags, and returned to Moore Hall at 7 o'clock to view the spread of sandwiches and Mrs Chilton's sausage rolls. We then waited for our guests to arrive and we were pleasantly surprised to see them in dresses and with their hair all made up; it was certainly different from seeing them walking around town in their school uniforms. I noticed one girl and made a beeline for her, asking if she would like a drink. She was very posh and said "That would be lovely, thank you." I went over to the freezer and opened the lid, but the smell nearly knocked me sideways. There was a smell of stinking fish on all the bottles. I slammed the lid closed and thought "What the hell am I going to do now?" Fortunately, in those days girls didn't drink out of the bottles, so I quickly took a Coke and went to the kitchen, washed and dried it, then poured it into a beaker and presented it to her with a big smile on my face (the smile of relief). I really had a great evening, dancing, chatting and watching the faces of the other boys as they opened the fishy chest freezer. I did go to my posh girl's house once after that but I can't remember ever seeing her again.

As I said before, on my days off from Howard's Judy and I spent time together, and with her being three years older than me and my hormones going wild it wasn't long before one afternoon in the woods I was initiated. Then it became quite a regular thing. I remember vividly one occasion when Dad was ill in hospital and Mum went to visit him, and by chance Judy called round to see me.

26

It wasn't long before we were in my bedroom. Time seems to fly by when you're having fun and the next thing I remember was the back door being opened and Mum calling my name. I frantically tried putting on my clothes as I scrambled downstairs. "Where is Judy?" were her first words. Naïvely I said, thinking she would believe me, "Upstairs looking at my magic books." Surprisingly, she didn't believe me and charged upstairs, and the next minute Judy came downstairs followed by Mum, who then held up a pair of frilly panties, saying "And whose are these?" Thinking what a bloody stupid question it was I felt like giving a bloody stupid answer back and saying "Mine", but then I thought, wisely, perhaps that wouldn't help matters, so I just kept quiet. Mum then turned her attention to Judy and, in no uncertain terms, told her to get out of the house and stay away from her son.

This was the start of the gradual decline of our relationship, but the thing that really sealed our demise was one day her stomach started to rumble and she tapped it saying "Quiet junior," then looked at me and smiled. The shock of the possible consequences of me being a father at sixteen made me think seriously of my future sexual activities, and the need for some protection was urgently required. In the early 60s, condoms were only usually available at the chemist or the barber's. The restricted availability of the 'Johnnie' resulted in a lot of unnecessary teenage pregnancies.

Buying your Johnnies from the barber was quite an interesting experience. After your haircut, the barber would brush you down, and then enquire "Anything for the weekend sir?" If the customer said "Yes please" the Barber would go to his drawer and put a packet of three condoms in a small brown envelope and then, like an MI5 agent, would pass them like a secret document into your hand. Being sixteen, I was never asked, and I never had the nerve to ask for the 'something for the weekend.' I'm sure I would not have ended up with condoms; it's more than likely they would have given me a jar of Brylcream. Whilst we were together Judy was very attentive to me and bought all my cigarettes and even bought me a lovely new guitar which I took to BB and played in a small trio.

27

CHAPTER 7

One day when I was hanging around in Moore Hall I heard music coming from at Etwall Hall, a sound I have never heard before; it was so loud and powerful that I just had to go and have a look. Peeping through the window I saw these four guys, three playing electric guitars and one on the drums. I knew them by sight but never really knew them to talk to. They were Howard Mansfield and his brother Morris, Bruce Turner and Ronnie Bullis, and were called The Emeralds. Little did I know what a prominent part Ronnie and Bruce would play in my future in the pop scene

Morrie Mansfield, Bruce Turner, Ronnie Bullis, Howard Mansfield (Ginger)

Morrie, Ginger and me at The Anton Arms 7th November 2015.

It was fortuitous as I was writing this book that Howard Mansfield (Ginger), who was the original guitarist with the Troggs, had just finished his story of the beginnings of the group. This I felt would be a fabulous insight into how 'The Troggs' and the name started. I contacted Ginger and asked him if I could include his story in my book and he kindly agreed. As these are his true feelings, in his own words, I have not altered them in any way.

* * *

How The Troggs Were Formed And Got Their Name

(Written by Howard Mansfield, AKA Ginger (Founder Member and Lead Guitarist)

Much has been written about the Troggs over the past years but no one seems to have written about how they first got together and got their name, as I'm the only original Trogg member left alive I thought it was about time I told this story as I remember it.

We first started when Ronnie Bullis, who was an old drummer friend of mine knocked on my door one day and asked me if I'd be interested in forming a new group with him as we'd both played together in a late fifties group called the Emeralds. At first I said no because I was married now and we had a baby son, Ronnie's answer to me was, I'm married too and I have a young son and not only that the group I was playing in has just folded and I'm left with a set of drums that I need to pay for. So after I'd had a talk with my wife Jacqui and got her approval I told Ronnie that I would consider it if I could get my work mate Reg who lived in the flat below me to join as well. Reg and I were both apprenticed bricklayers and worked on the same firm together, we were also in the same class at school where I remember him singing all the time just the same way as he still did at work. Ronnie and I both went down stairs and knocked on his door and asked Reg if he would be interested in joining up with us, his answer was a very quick yes but then he said to me I can't play anything can I, I told him don't worry about it I'll teach you how to play the bass guitar and that was that, sorted!

The next thing we had to do was buy some music gear so a trip up to London's Charing Cross road was next on the cards, unfortunately for us good instruments cost a lot of money which we didn't have, so Ronnie came up with the bright idea of asking somebody he knew if they might want to manage us and help us out with our money problem, this guy's name was Stan Phillips who was a local businessman that owned a shop fitting company and also the Copper Kettle tearooms in Andover's high-street, the tearooms also had a large reception room above it which would be ideal for us to practice in. Because Ronnie new Stan best of all we pushed him to the front and plucked up courage to go and see him. Our proposal was that we would make him an equal member of the group if he would manage us and helped us buy our music gear. This of course was a bit of a long shot, but to our astonishment he actually loved the idea and agreed to it as long as we took on the HP ourselves he would make all the initial payments for us until we started earning money from our gigs. Stan's friends thought he was totally nuts when he told them, but Stan actually told them, when you get to our age don't get yourself a sports car to young feel young get yourselves a rock group.

Stan lent us one of his works vans and we then headed up to London's Charing Cross road to Lou Davis which was a music shop I'd used before. I bought myself a second-hand Fender Strat and a Selmer Thunderbird 100 watt amp, Reg bought a Framus bass and a Selmer Thunderbird 100 watt bass amp, we also bought a Selmer 100 watt PA outfit plus three Bayer mics with stands and a Watkins copycat echo. We started practicing in the evenings at the Copper Kettle and soon got noticed by people walking by who always seemed to ask if there was a dance going on upstairs. Although practising gave us a chance to get used to playing together there was something missing and we soon all agreed that what we really needed was a good lead singer so we decided to hold some auditions and advertise them in the front window of the Copper Kettle. We had several people turn up that night but there was one guy who really stood out above the rest and was really eager to join us, his name was Dave Wright and as a bonus he also played the guitar and harmonica. Dave was a little younger than us and already had long hair and a great personality, he fitted in perfectly.

So now another trip up to Lou Davis was on the cards to get Dave's gear sorted out, he chose himself a Gretsch Tennessean guitar and a Selmer Thunderbird 100 watt amp and also another Bayer mic and stand, we also had to buy another Watkins copycat echo as each unit only had two inputs, I also wanted to change my Fender Stratocaster for an Epiphone Casino because Keith Richards was playing one at that time and it sounded great, Reg wanted to change his Framus Bass for a Burns Bison Bass and not to feel left out Ronnie exchanged his Premier Drum kit for a Ludwig set.

It was on this trip to London that we actually got our name, whilst driving up there we picked up two girls who were hitchhiking to London on the A30; they both were students at Basingstoke College. They could see all our music gear in the back of the van and asked if we were a group, obviously we said yes then came the question, what do you call yourselves and we had to say to them we haven't got a name yet, so one of the girls said why don't you call yourselves the Grotty Troggs to which we all replied at the same time fuck off we're not grotty and it was touch and go whether we dumped them back on the A30 or not, only kidding.

On our way home after we'd dropped the two girls off and sorted out our business at Lou Davis's Dave said that name the those girls said might be ok if we leave the word grotty out and just use the Trogg part, we all had a think about it and decided that it might be alright providing we find out first exactly what a Trogg was. Apparently it's short for troglodyte, which according to the World English Dictionary its prehistoric person thought to have lived in a cave, and so on that day the Troggs were born.

Back in Andover we set-to practicing all the songs we knew and with Dave's new input we expanded our repertoire to more of an R&B type of music which seemed to go down really well with the fans. I remember a few days after we came back from London Stan Phillips asked us to come down to the Copper Kettle as he had a big surprise for us and it certainly was because sat in the car park was a brand spanking new light blue Bedford Van and on both sides of it painted in big white letters our name "The Troggs" we were all completely gobsmacked and could hardly believe it.

At that particular time all our gigs were fairly local but it wasn't long before our name got known and we started getting much better bookings with more money but the trouble with that was, because we still had to go to work every day, the further away the gigs were the it harder it was for us to get to there and get setup. So we decided to try and get a roadie but it had to be someone with a good idea of what it all entailed. I can't remember exactly who came up with his name but this guy not only didn't mind doing most of the driving but also knew how to set our gear up, his name was Johnny Gardener and he really was a great guy to work with. Getting Johnny as a roadie was a result for us and it made things a lot easier, but as more and more bookings came in we were unable to cope with the pressure of working all day and doing gigs in the evening, so Stan Phillips told us to pack in our day jobs and he would cover our wages on the understanding that when our bookings became slack we would work for him in his shop fitting firm, of course we all jumped at the chance.

In Andover at that time we only had one serious rival group to contend with and that was The Ten Feet Five which consisted of John Walker on Drums, Pete Staples on Bass, Chris Penfound on Guitar and vocals, Chris Britton on Lead Guitar and Dave Smith on Lead vocals.

CHAPTER 8

As I mentioned before, hearing The Emeralds had a real effect on me and it was a big surprise when Bruce Turner, their singer, later approached me and said he was starting his own group and would I like to join. This was in 1959 when I was fifteen and up until then I had only previously been in a skiffle group and a trio in the BB with acoustic guitars.

Bruce worked as a dental technician, and next door was a butcher's shop where Arthur Smart worked; they became friends and Bruce asked him if he would like to join his band. Arthur had never played a musical instrument in his life, but like Ginger and Reg with The Troggs, Bruce said he would show Arthur what to do. They went the local music shop Sainsbury and Fisher and came away with a Rossetti bass. After many days at Bruce's mum's house he learnt 'FBI' by The Shadows.

Prior to playing with The Emeralds Bruce was in another group called The Bandits which was a skiffle group and their washboard player was John Walker. Bruce said John was the best washboard player he had ever heard and had since progressed onto a drum kit. John would be the fourth member of Bruce's new group which was called The Senators. Unlike Ginger we didn't have the sponsorship of Stan Phillips or parents with money. The only help we got was from Bruce's father who had a market stall selling crockery and he let us use his van. Bruce had a Hofner Colorama guitar, I had an acoustic with a pickup and Arthur the Rossetti bass. Rossetti were very cheap guitars that were made in Eindhoven Holland by Egmont and were about 10% of the price of a Fender or Gibson; still, they were affordable to most people and even Paul and George started off with Egmont. They were distributed in Great Britain under the name of Rossetti. Arthur had the Bass 7. Our

34

biggest problem was getting amplifiers that we could afford. Bruce already had his but neither Arthur or myself had one; we didn't even have a PA system or microphone. Arthur being an apprentice butcher, and me being a sausage and faggot maker, and both of us being smokers, meant we never had any spare cash for expensive equipment.

After a while we gradually got some amplification together complete with speakers. I remember my amplifier was just a chassis with three knobs, a transformer and some valves; I also used television cable with jack plugs as a guitar lead. The speakers were not in cabinets and had to be propped up against a chair. The cables that went into the amplifier were held in the terminals by matchsticks as were the main cables to the amplifier. In retrospect it's a wonder that nobody ever got electrocuted, as often you could hear a loud humming noise coming from the speakers when you touched the strings on your instruments.

I remember one time watching Bruce singing through a Reslo ribbon mike and sparks jumping across to his lips. It is quite frightening to think of now, with all the electrical regulations and the PAT testing, the risks we took when playing and enjoying our music. We practised about two nights a week, sometimes at Bruce's mother's house and sometimes at my house. I was still working at the butcher's and my relationship with Judy had virtually run its course.

One day when I was walking through the fish department I noticed on the marble display slab a 4' shark beautifully displayed and surrounded with prawns, shrimps, scallops and other fish. I was so fascinated by this killer of the sea with his evil eyes and the snare of those vicious teeth I just kept going back to have another look. I eventually decided to ask Des, the manager, what he was going to do with it at the end of the day. He said, "Dump it in the bin, why?" I said, "Can I have it?" He chuckled and said, "Yes if you want it."

At 5 o'clock I collected the shark ready to take him home, but I did find it hard getting him on my bicycle as he was so slippery. I managed to get his head on the handlebars and his tail on the saddle. So off I went through the yard and up Union Street into the recreation ground on my way home. I certainly turned a few heads as people walked by, but halfway home I thought, 'What the hell am I going to do with him when I get him home?' It then dawned on me that this was not such a good idea. Turning the bicycle around with the slippery carcass on the handlebars was quite a struggle, but eventually I managed it and was quickly on my way back to Howard's before they closed. The thought of them being shut, and me stuck outside with a 4' shark, was a bit worrying, and the only other place I thought I could get rid of him in that event would have been the Town River. Fortunately, the yard gates were still open so I quickly pushed the bike over to the big waste bins, lifted him off the bike and slid him in. Feeling very relieved, but a bit stupid, I cycled home, only for my mother to ask why I stank of fish. I told her somebody in the fish department threw some fishy water over me. I can't remember if I ever told her the truth.

One day whilst I was making sausage meat the machine just stopped. I reported it to Bill my boss, who called in the electricity company to fix it. An electrician arrived with a meter and some screwdrivers and I thought, what a marvellous job that is, and I decided that was what I would like to do, so when I got home that evening I told my dad. He was very pleased and decided to make enquiries with different electrical firms in the town to see if they needed an apprentice. I had an interview with F Found and Son at Weyhill and was lucky enough to be offered an apprenticeship. When I told Bill, my boss, I was leaving he said he was very sorry and if I stayed I could go to Technical College to learn butchery, but the thought of walking around with a meter and some screwdrivers appealed to me much more and I decided to take Mr Found's offer. It came as a bit of a shock to discover that being an electrician was not just carrying a meter and some screwdrivers: it was more like chopping boxes on a building site, crawling through dirty roofs, under floors and getting less money than I was earning at the butcher's, but I was determined to stay with it and finish my five years' apprenticeship. This was a wise decision as even today I have a trade that I can always fall back on to earn a living.

My life was very busy, but enjoyable, being an apprentice electrician and playing in The Senators, who eventually had enough numbers to start gigging. This was mostly in pubs like The Boot at Verham Dene and The Star at Weyhill Road. When we started getting paid for the gigs we had a little bit more money and gradually upgraded our equipment. Bruce bought a new Vox Consort guitar and I bought his old Colorama, and we also paid someone to build cabinets to put the speakers in. (See photo)

Travelling in Bruce's dad's Bedford van was not a comfortable experience as there were only two seats in the front and an old car bench seat at the back. The passenger seat was not fixed. I remember Bruce picking me up for a gig one evening. As we were late, I threw my guitar in the back of the van and jumped into the passenger seat; Bruce accelerated away and I found myself in a pile at the back of the van amongst the equipment. All good fun.

Bruce couldn't use his dad's van for some reason one day, so Arthur had to borrow one from his boss, which stank of meat, but got us to the gig and back. That night Bruce had to go somewhere after the gig and asked if we could look after the day's takings from his crockery stall. The money was kept in an OXO tin and he asked if we would drop it off at his house. Around midnight we took the van back to the butcher's and walked through the town clutching the OXO tin containing wads of £5 and £10 notes. We were approached and stopped by a copper who asked us what we had in the tin. We told him the true story but he didn't believe it and took us to the police station where we were held for two hours while somebody went to Bruce's house to check us out. Thankfully, Bruce was already back home and confirmed our story so we were then released.

On stage we wore charcoal grey suits, because most people had one, it being the standard colour for most occasions, with a white shirt, so the only thing we had to buy was bow ties. We also played at the Teen and 20, a club that Bruce and his girlfriend June ran; this was held at a hall at the back of the bus station and was always well attended, so much so that they had to move to the Fiesta Hall which was a bigger venue. In 1963 the manager told Bruce and June they could no longer use the Fiesta Hall because the girls' stiletto heels were damaging the floor, plus he didn't approve of some of the lewd words the groups used. So The Teen and 20 Rock and Twist Club moved to Upper Clatford Village Hall for a while before it eventually packed up.

Sometimes we would play at the Fiesta and also go dancing there when we weren't performing. One evening we saw a group called The Redwoods and the line-up consisted of Chris Britton, that chap I saw coming off the rugby field all those years ago, Chris Penfound, who I knew vaguely from my school days, Dave Glover, John Hayward. They had a very good sound and better equipment than we had and a very enthusiastic following. They were like another Andover group, The Strangers, who were the top group in Andover. They relied a lot on instrumentals playing numbers by The Shadows and The Vipers rather than vocals and it wasn't until The Redwoods brought in Dave Smith, who also sang in The Strangers under the name of Dave DuVal, and earlier with The Emeralds, that they could vary their programme.

The Senators Arthur Smart, John Walker, Bruce Turner and me

The Redwoods Chris Britten, John Hayward, Dave Smith, Chris Penfound and Dave Glover

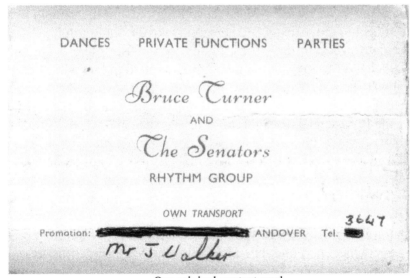

Our original contact card

In the mid-to-late 60s bands were still popular, i.e. trumpets, saxophones etc, so the evening was split between a band and the 'up and coming' new type of music from the pop groups.

In 1961 The Andover Variety Club had organised a show at St Anne's Hall and they asked The Senators to perform. This was quite a different gig for us as there were other acts and a sit down audience. On the bill were comedians Braxton and Cook, singer John Hanson, dancer Jean Wardell and a local female dancing troupe called Dominoes. Arthur started to date Yvonne, one of the girls in the dance troupe, who he eventually married a year later. I started to date Jean, whose father was the local police photographer. One day I was at her house when a call came through from the police saying there was a very nasty accident at Weyhill Road. Her dad grabbed his camera and asked if I would like to go along, so thinking that I would be a part of the important crash team I agreed.

On arriving at the accident I saw this green 3.0 ltr Jag wrapped round a tree. As it was pitch black he asked me if I would to take a lamp and stand by the wreckage, so he could aim his camera at it, then I could move away and he would take the photograph. He told me not to look in the car as a body was still in there. I gingerly walked over to the vehicle then turned around to face him. I don't know if he was winding me up but he kept saying "Move back nearer to the car" "Move to the left" "Move to the right" a bit nearer to the car... and I thought for Christ's sake hurry up! I was so relieved when he said "That will do," and as quick as a flash I moved away from the car so he could take his photographs.

Jean lived the other side of town from me and I usually had to walk home, a walk that took me by St Mary's Church. Many a time I would say to myself, "Tonight I'm really going to walk through that graveyard," which would cut some time off my journey, but I always chickened out. The night after that car accident there was no way I was going to attempt that shortcut, even the walk home in the dark was spooky. Jean was quite a celebrity in the town: one year she was the Carnival Queen, and she also had her own school of dancing. She did tell me once she wanted to be a ballerina but got top heavy - I did come to realise later that my taste in girls would be the 'top heavy' type.

With most girlfriends when you're young the relationship usually fizzles out and you both go your different ways; this happened with us, for no particular reason, other than being young and wanting to move on to different things.

But it wasn't long before I had a new girlfriend. One Friday night John and I went to the Fiesta Hall to see what crumpet was about, and we both noticed two girls dancing together who looked really classy. After agreeing we would ask them for a dance I told John which one I fancied and he didn't mind as the other one was just as lovely. After approaching them and asking if we could join in, I came out with the usual chat, and asked, "What's your name?" She replied, "Hilary." After dancing for a while I asked, "What you do in your spare time?" and she replied "I like to go riding." I thought Pete, we are in the money here, then asked her how she was getting home, and she said, "My father is going to pick me up." I mentioned I was in a band called The Senators and we were playing at The Bell next Saturday would she like to come along; she said, "Okay." At the end of the dance I walked her to the door where a man in a Ford Prefect, wearing a cloth cap, was waiting for her; this I thought must be the butler or somebody from the household...

Well I started to see a lot of Hilary and John started seeing Vivian her friend. We even went over and had a ride on the horses; they actually belonged to the farmer and not them, but this didn't matter, or even that they lived in a semi in Enham Village. They were good-looking and great fun, which extended to letting John and me get on the horses that they knew would fight: it wasn't long after getting on their backs that they started to rear, bite and kick, causing both of us to dismount a bit bloody quick. I hated horses, even the way they looked at me - it was as if they were saying "I'm going to get you." Later I did ride a horse in Texas, and a polo pony that nearly killed me as a publicity stunt, but I will tell you about that later.

Being in a band seemed to help getting dates with the girls but when I was seeing Hilary frequently I didn't want to bother with anybody else. I bought a 1947 Morris 8 car from Bruce's girlfriend June so I could take John, Vivian and Hilary out. The Morris 8 was a very basic car with no heater, three forward gears, one small windscreen wiper and indicator arms that would flick out from the door pillars (sometimes) to indicate a left or right turn. If they didn't operate you had to bang the door pillar with your fist to dislodge them.

The band went from strength to strength playing in Hampshire and the West Country. We could even afford proper stage clothes and went to London to Anallo and David and purchased silver crocodile effect boots and midnight blue glitter stage jackets from Cecil Gee. We wore these when Jess Conrad appeared at the Fiesta Hall, 9th July 1963 (see photo). One of our regular gigs was the Country Club in Tidworth where we had a big following. The owner was so pleased with the increased number of customers we pulled in that he was continually buying us pints. Sometimes I could have five pints on a tray by my amp and by the end of the evening we were all usually pissed. I remember once playing my bass slumped in a chair on stage unable to stand properly. One night Reg Ball turned up and when we had our break he asked, "Can I have a go on a guitar?" He sat on the stage and played a few chords.

Playing at JV's North Virginia 2014, after a reunion with John and Arthur

Jess Conrad with The Senators at the Fiesta Hall

Arthur, John and I visiting John who now lives in Washington in June 2014

Bruce Turner and I at The Anton Arms, November 7th 2015

Reg had not been in a band yet but I could see that he would love to be on stage. Little did I know then how dramatically both our lives would change a few years later. The Country Club was always a very good gig for us as it was local so Hilary and Vivian could come and see us, but Hilary's dad would always pick them up at 11.30. After the girls had gone home we would pack up our gear and make our way to Penton Corner café, just outside Andover, for coffee, and Bruce would do his party trick, stuffing a whole Walls steak and kidney pie in his mouth in one go just like a python eating a small mammal. He was always the showman.

CHAPTER 9

Life has a funny way of kicking you in the balls when things seem to be going well. I was seeing Hilary, had an apprenticeship, was playing in the band: life was just fine. However, in September 1963 it all started to go wrong. One evening we were booked for a gig somewhere in Wiltshire, I can't remember where, but what I can remember is Bruce producing a brand-new Fender Stratocaster guitar out of a case. This really blew our minds, as it was one of the best guitars you could get, but our excitement was soon dashed when he said this would be his last gig with us. Apparently, he'd been asked to join another band called The Trendsetters, made up from hand-picked musicians from around the southern area to make a supergroup. This left us devastated and right in the shit as Bruce was the singer, the lead guitar player and had the van; to replace all that would certainly take a lot of effort and a lot of time.

This was my first experience of a group member leaving and I found it very unsettling. Later I found out that this is common with groups and would also happen to me in a big and devastating way. After getting through the gig Bruce drove us home, dropped us off and said goodbye and that was the end of my first band.

I didn't know if we could get the band going again. I did ask Arthur and John and I can't remember if they were keen or not, but on doing my research for this book I did find an advert in the Andover Advertiser 11th Oct 1963 saying The Senators required a lead guitar so we must have been thinking of trying to carry on. As Arthur was already married and had a baby girl and John had a steady girlfriend as well (not Vivian as they had since gone their separate ways), I didn't know how dedicated they would be to starting a new band. I was still seeing Hilary and without the group

I spent a lot more time seeing her. In retrospect I think this must have put a lot of pressure on her and restricted her freedom and it wasn't long before we parted company. This I found very difficult to handle on top of not having the group; I can honestly say that was about the worst time of my young life. I just did not know what to do with myself: the group and my girlfriend were my life. Also, Hilary had found a new boyfriend whose parents were quite wealthy and, to make matters worse, he drove a nice Wolsey 1500 car with a heater, carpets and walnut dashboard. This was way out of my league.

Without seeing Hilary and not having a group I had a lot of spare time on my hands so I started to go out drinking for something to do and to drown my sorrows. This went on for quite a while until one day I thought this was getting me nowhere and I started to worry about the future and the way my life was going, or more to the point, not going. I decided to join the Merchant Navy and made arrangements to visit Southampton Docks to find out what jobs were available - maybe I could be an electrician's mate on board ship and see the world. These thoughts stopped me dwelling on what I had lost, and made me focus more on what I was going to do in the future. Fortunately, I didn't need to take that trip to Southampton as my luck was beginning to change again.

Chris Britton, the lead guitarist with the Ten Feet Five, formerly the Redwoods, approached me and said that their bass player was leaving and asked me if I would like to take his place. I said I would love to, but told him I was rhythm guitar and I didn't have a bass. He said, "Don't worry, Dave Glover said you could borrow his until you get one."

The thought of playing in another band filled me with a lot of excitement, but also apprehension, as I had never played the bass and knew I had a lot of learning to do. This I didn't mind as the Ten Feet Five had good gear and Dave Smith, the singer who had recently joined, was the best around; plus they had a van, albeit a rusty old Morris J2 that was used by the Redwoods. To advertise the group, Chris had painted a big foot on both sides of the van and the name of the group. Somebody once said to me "Is that a butcher's van you drive?" I replied "No, why?" "Because it looks like a pork chop and five chipolatas." I had to tell him that it was a group van and the picture was supposed to represent a footprint, but looking at it I could see what he meant.

Being back in a band gave my life some purpose. That might sound a bit melodramatic to some people, but when you've been in a band for four years and it has taken up the bulk of your spare time, the loss is similar to packing up smoking or somebody giving up drink. I know because I've experienced all three, and being without the band I found by far the most depressing. The line-up of the new group was Chris Britton lead guitar, Chris Penfound rhythm guitar, Johnny Hayward drums, Dave Smith vocals and me on bass guitar.

Ten Feet Five Promotional handout

We all got on very well but Johnny Hayward sometimes seemed to be unhappy with things, and one day he announced that he wanted to train to be a teacher, which would mean going to teachers' training college. Pre-empting his plans we had invited John Walker, my mate from the Senators, to be our drummer. With John Walker on the drums that completed the line-up of one of Andover's most popular groups. We could all sing a bit, enabling us to move away from all those instrumentals that The Redwoods and The Strangers did and do more vocal harmonies; this was right up my street as my favourite groups were The Beatles and The Four Seasons.

Dave was an old trooper, having sung in most of the bands in Andover, including The Emeralds, doing mostly R&B, so we could now do a very varied show and, even better, Chris Penfound was fantastic on the harmonica. From being so depressed a few months earlier I was really on cloud nine in my new band. It wasn't long before we started doing gigs and, believe it or not, our first gig was at Moore Hall, my old nursery and BB headquarters, (no, the smell of fish had long gone). We did a lot of gigs in the West Country; this might as well have been called the Wild West as often there were big fights with chairs and bodies flying around and girls screaming.

We always found it safer to keep playing and enjoy the action from our vantage point on the stage, leaving the bouncers to pile in and sort it out. At one dance in Wiltshire the people were packed in tightly and at the end of the evening we found several condoms on the dance floor; I wonder what dance they were doing? I thought maybe the Hokey Pokey; maybe you can think of a dance more appropriate!

Going home one night from a gig the van started to misfire and found it increasingly difficult getting up hills, so we to stopped to check if the fuel was getting into the carburettor. After we had taken the fuel pipe off the strong smell of piss and petrol wafted around. We had to assume that some jealous boyfriend had pissed in the petrol tank. However, after discharging a large quantity of the offending mixture from the pipe to the carburettor, the engine started up and sounded much healthier. Relieved, we continued home.

As I mentioned the J2 was very rusty, especially where the body met the floor, with a long slit down one side. In the winter, there would always be a cold draught on your legs. Sometimes girls would ask if we could give them a lift home and we were always very happy to oblige, not that we wanted to try anything on, only to sit them on the floor by the rust holes to stop the draught coming in. We laughed when they said "It's a bit draughty in here ain't it?"

Travelling in the back of the J2 in the winter was not much fun as there was only an old bench seat from a car that was not secured. The heat from the heater in the front never really reached us in the back so it was a case of coats, scarves and gloves. Although at times it was cold and fairly uncomfortable, I do look back with great fondness on these memories, like driving home at two in the morning with the moon shining, the frost on the grass and the mist hovering in the valleys, pulling up at an all-night cafe ordering breakfast, coffee, having a fag and enjoying the usual banter of groups, i.e. taking the mickey out of each other.

Pork chop and chipolata van

Travelling around in the summer was much better as we played a lot of seaside resorts. One of our favourites was the pier at Southsea. I remember doing a double gig there on the Saturday and Sunday, so rather than go home Saturday night we slept in the van on Portsdown Hill overlooking the sea. As you can imagine this was quite a squeeze for all five of us and the equipment, so John decided that he would sleep outside on the grass giving a bit more room for the rest of us. Dave decided to sleep at the front lying across the two seats with his head resting on the door. This was okay until John decided in the early hours of the morning that he was too cold and wanted to get back in the van; he slid the door open trapping Dave's head. Dave jumped up shouting "What the fuck are you doing?" John, standing there with his blanket over his arm, said, "Can I come in? It's cold out here." Dave's reply was "No, piss off." I think Dave did relent in the end and let him in, but I don't think we got much sleep after that interruption.

CHAPTER 10

When I was an electrician I worked with a man called Lance Barrett who was very 'switched on' (no pun intended) at seizing an opportunity and then getting the most out of it. He was smartly dressed, had a very warm personality and was well spoken. He realised the potential of the latest trends, running dances and bingo halls around Andover, and he started a booking agency called Lance Barrett Agency; he gave us quite a lot of bookings. He had links with an Agency called Avenue Artists in Southampton and they kept us very busy around Andover, the West Country and Southampton. Lance must have seen something in us because one day he said he would like to be our manager and he drew up a contract. As some of us were underage he went to see all our parents to get their consent and signatures. Having Lance as manager was the best thing we ever did.

All the money we earned was put into an account and by saving we could buy the best equipment, i.e. Vox AC 30, Vox AC 50 bass amp for me and Vox PA columns. We also got rid of the rusty old van complete with pork chop and chipolatas painted on the side and purchased the J2 minibus with windows and comfortable seats in the back. We went to Martin Loveridge, a local high-class tailor, to be measured and fitted with suits.

With Lance being connected to Avenue Artists, we were now getting bookings farther afield and creating quite a name for ourselves. Some of the bill posters read "By popular demand the 10 feet 5." Lance had big hopes for us not only playing gigs but also having a hit record, so with the songs of local songwriters he booked us into Hamilton Electronics recording studio in Southampton, where we recorded some demos. It was about this time that Bruce Turner and The Trendsetters released their first single, 'In A Big Way', in April 1964, but this did not give Bruce the result that he so desperately wanted and even after more releases with the supergroup he never achieved all that he hoped for. However, Bruce did have another bite of the cherry with The Loot, another group from Andover made up of lads from Men Friday, The Troggs, The Redwoods and Bruce from The Senators. The Loot, Stan Phillips and White Cottage held some of the most bizarre and unbelievable stories that I tell later.

At Martin Loveridge Andover – measured and fitted with our new suits

The music scene throughout the country was beginning to change and because groups like Pete Mystery and the Strangers, who for many years had led the way in Andover, had not changed their style, they found their popularity waning and finally disbanded. This left the Troggs and the Ten Feet Five as the two major bands in Andover. The Ten Feet Five covered mostly the more popular music and the Troggs were R&B. With Lance being our manager and Stan Phillips being the Troggs' manager there was always healthy competition which gave both camps the drive to be the most successful.

Stan realised that Lance having a booking agency would give the Ten Feet Five an advantage with bookings around the area. He told Lance that if he didn't treat the Troggs as equals with bookings then he would start his own agency and put Lance out of business. I did feel that this was a bit unfair as the Troggs hadn't been going that long and most of their gigs were playing every Thursday night at the R&B club in the Copper Kettle, which Stan owned. I did go down to see them play once and was very impressed with their sound, especially when Dave Wright did 'Tell Me,' a Stones number. This is still one of my favourite songs and I love singing it to this day. Our popularity grew so much that we started to get booked in large ballrooms like Swindon Locarno, the Pier at Southsea, Boscombe Arcade, Winchester Lido and Southampton Pier.

Playing at Swindon Locarno

One night we played at Boscombe Arcade and John and I chatted up a couple of local girls and arranged to see them in their car after we packed away the gear. After chatting with them for a while and pulling their legs about giving us a lift back to Andover, we heard Dave shout, "Are you two coming?" John jumped out of the car and went across to talk to the lads, then returned to the car. To my amazement the van drove off. In panic I said, "Where are they going John?" He replied, "Don't worry, Pete," then winked, and continued chatting and teasing the girls about giving us a lift back to Andover. By this time the girls were really panicking, thinking they would be stuck with us now the group van had gone, but John said with bravado, "Don't worry, just drop us up on the dual carriageway we'll be alright," so I decided to play the same macho game and agreed: "We'll be all right, don't worry about us."

The girls were getting quite concerned, so to ease their worries we assured them again: "Just take us up to the dual carriageway." So after a bit of a grope we said goodbye. As they drove away I turned to John and said, "Where's the van then?" and to my utter amazement he said, "They've gone."

"GONE! Didn't you arrange to meet them somewhere?"

"No," he said.

"How the bloody hell are we going to get home then?"

"Walk," he said.

"What, fifty miles at one o'clock in the morning with no buses or cars about?"

The only comment he could come up with was "You will laugh about this in years to come." My thoughts were not on the years to come but the mess we were in - all because he wanted a kiss and cuddle. As for my part, I can't think of any sexual favours I would have considered so attractive that I would be willing to be left stranded fifty miles away from home at one o'clock in the morning; but this was the reality of our situation and we had no alternative but to start walking.

John decided that if we sang as we walked, the time would pass much quicker. We gave up singing after half an hour, and the odd passing vehicle had totally ignored our frantic thumbing. I was getting quite concerned, and after three hours and nine miles, real panic started to creep in and I began to acknowledge that if things didn't improve we could spend a long cold night... I just didn't know where. But our luck suddenly changed: we saw the reflection of car lights behind us, and as it got nearer we frantically started to thumb and thank God it stopped. We rushed over and the bloke said, "I'm going to Winchester if that's any help." We just couldn't wait and got straight into that lovely warm car.

He had his girlfriend with him and when we told them how we had got ourselves in this predicament they found it very amusing. By now I was also beginning to see the funny side of it, since I didn't realise then that the worst was still to come. After they dropped us off in Winchester at about 3.30am we thanked them and set off on our homeward journey to John's house at Chilbolton about ten miles away. I don't know if it was because we had left the warmth of the car, but it did feel a lot colder and I only had a cardigan, so John lent me his scarf. We thought our luck had changed and we would get a lift on the last leg, but this was wishful thinking as not a single vehicle passed us. Not only that, it started to rain, and John began to complain about his Cuban heeled boots hurting him.

As we reached the outskirts of Chilbolton, the dawn chorus started and the darkness began to evaporate. Suddenly out of the blue John fell in the hedge crying "I can't go on" because his feet were hurting him so much. This was an unwelcome problem as we were so close to his home, so he tried walking in his socks, but stepping on so many stones he soon realised that it was less painful wearing his boots. We finally reached his house and quietly crept into the kitchen to make a cup of tea. I could see the sheer look of relief on his face that he was home and his bed was just upstairs, but I still had another six miles to go. Luckily John had a 50cc Honda bike and he said I could use to complete my journey.

Those six miles were for me the worst part of our epic night/morning. I was wet, tired, hungry, and cold, and travelling at fifty miles an hour on a motorbike with the wind biting at my face made every mile seem like five and every minute feel like ten. Arriving home about 7.30am I parked John's bike around the back and staggered through the lounge and into the passage, only to meet my mum coming down the stairs. "You're late," she said. "Do you want some breakfast?" Not wanting to discuss the night's disaster I just said "No" and passed her on the stairs, went to my room, kicked off my shoes, fell into bed and stayed there until four o'clock in the afternoon.

Not all our gigs were in ballrooms. We did have some unusual ones like playing at Broadmoor Hospital. Chris's uncle was in charge there, and invited us to play to the patients and then to the prison warders' families in the evening. This was in their club on the opposite side of the road from the hospital.

After a brief tour of the hospital we set up our gear in the large hall, with the help of some of the low-risk patients. We were served lunch by the patients and after a cup of tea and a fag we were ready and made our way to the stage not knowing what to expect from our 'captive' audience. The hall was packed with male and female patients sitting and waiting in anticipation to hear live rock 'n' roll.

After we were introduced, they were asked to give us a warm welcome and we jumped up on stage. Not knowing what sort of reception we would get, or what to say, we went straight into 'Johnny B Goode'. To our great relief this got them clapping and singing and set the tone for the whole show. It's quite strange that we were playing to some of the most dangerous and, in some cases, most evil people of our society, but they all seemed quite normal, especially one very attractive girl who was waving her arms in the air and wiggling her hips from side to side and singing along with us. Afterwards, I enquired with one of the wardens why she was in the hospital. He said she was at another prison having breakfast when the girl next to her used up all the milk, so she picked up the empty milk bottle and smashed her across the head with it.

When we finished the patients were clapping and shouting for more as we left the stage. Watching the film of 'Johnny Cash at Folsom Prison', one of America's most notorious penitentiaries, where he sang country and western to prisoners, makes me ponder that we have played in one of Britain's most notorious hospitals singing rock 'n' roll. Because it was a mental hospital we were not allowed to walk around, or even go to the toilet, without a warden being with us. I remember going to the gents accompanied by a warden and whilst standing at the urinal a male patient who was standing beside me said, pointing to the chrome air fresheners above the urinal, "They're microphones - be careful what you say."

In the evening we set out our gear in the wardens' social club across the road to entertain the wardens' families. This was an enjoyable gig, but the only thing that spoiled the day was having my new imitation sheepskin coat stolen from our dressing room (they say there are more criminals out than there are in).

Now that we were an established group Lance decided the time was right for us to have a record released, so yet again, with local songwriters John Porter, Terry King and John Clayton, we rehearsed some of their songs: 'Send Me No more Loving' and 'Baby's Back In Town'. Lance then contacted Harold Geller who was an arranger/conductor and worked with the BBC; he also had contacts in the record industry. Lance asked if he would be interested in being our producer, which he agreed to. We let Harold book the recording studio, then after the session asked him if he would make copies and, through his contacts in the record industry, try to get the record released.

The day of the recording, at Ryemuse, South Molton Street, Mayfair, was a very exciting time for us and we recorded all day Saturday and Sunday, bagging six tracks. All we had to do now was wait and hope that Harold could get our record released. We eventually heard that Phillips had agreed to release it. This, apparently, was not because the record was that good, but because they needed to release so many records per month and ours was just to make up the shortfall for that month. To have your record heard on the radio for the first time was quite a strange feeling; also on the bill posters we could say 'The 10 feet 5: Fontana recording artists.' As we were the first group in Andover to have a record released, we were invited to have tea with the Mayor and Mayoress. Not knowing how successful our record would be we just carried on with gigging and doing our day jobs.

By now, having completed my apprenticeship, I had left Found's, and I went to work for another electrical firm, but they went bust, so I signed on at the labour exchange and was sent to Enham Industries, a large factory situated in Enham Alamain, three miles from Andover that made furniture for the government. It was a bit embarrassing as Hilary's father was the floor manager there and I was not employed as an electrician but worked on the router, a machine which cut holes in wooden blocks. I had to push a foot pedal down, release it, then put the block on a pallet. This was mind boggling boring work, so much so that one day I picked up a block as I was looking at a girl walk by and took my eye off what I was doing. The cutter ran across three of my fingers just nicking them. Even now when I think how I could have lost three fingers, I still feel my toes curl up.

I just prayed that our record would be successful so I could jack this job in. Unfortunately, our hopes and dreams gradually ebbed away as week after week there was no sign of it entering the charts. This really affected the whole group, and for my part the means of getting away from my boring job. I would sit in the group van at lunch time and listen to Workers' Playtime on the radio, with guest groups like The Honeycombs, The Apple Jacks and The Searchers and dream if only that could be me. The failure of the record to make it in the charts did cause despondency in the group, a despondency which was frighteningly familiar to me. One Sunday Lance called a meeting at his house to talk about future plans following the failure of the record, but Chris P was now getting concerned about his future and would rather invest his time in his job as a proof reader. Dave, who was recently married, said Gail, his wife, didn't want him to carry on playing in the band. John said that if Dave was leaving, then there would be no point in carrying on so he decided he wanted to go as well. My nightmare of not having a group had returned and to make matters worse, I had a shitty boring job as well.

Although this was a serious setback, things were not so disastrous as my previous experience with The Senators, as Chris Britton still wanted to carry on, and we had equipment, we had a van, and we had a manager/agent; all we had to do was find a drummer and maybe a singer. I also didn't have the anguish of losing a girlfriend as this time I didn't have one; I was just playing the field. One of the big problems when a group breaks up is how the equipment is to be dispersed: does the singer take the PA and all the other members take their own amps? Which, in reality, belong to the group; and what about the new van, what should happen to that? I don't think there are any hard and fast rules regarding this as every group situation is different, and the solution usually ends up being decided by the feelings of each group member.

Star and Garter, Andover 2015. Me, John Walker and Chris Penfound standing

Prior to the group breaking up we did a gig at Boscombe Arcade ballrooms. Unfortunately our drummer couldn't make it, which left us a bit of a problem, but fortunately the other group on the bill, The Daisies, said that if their drummer agreed we could use him. Thankfully he did. His name was Tony Taylor, and he recalls the night very well. He played two hours for The Daisies and a further two hours for us. Not surprisingly, he was completely knackered at the end of it. We were so grateful to Tony and when we were looking for our new drummer Chris immediately thought of him. We contacted him and told him of our predicament and asked if he would like to join us. He agreed, but had no means of transport and he lived in Winchester. This was not problem, as I had the van, and Chris had a Wolseley car, so we could pick him up and drop him off. It's quite ironic that I had completely forgotten about Tony playing in our group until he contacted me and told me the story. The only thing that I could remember was every so often dropping somebody off at Parchment Street, Winchester and that turned out to be Tony.

It's quite frightening that I'd completely forgotten four or five months of gigging in a band - and that's without being on drugs - but thankfully the more I heard, the more I remembered. Tony recalled that most of our gigs were around the Andover, Winchester and Southampton areas, and amazingly he had also kept our old playlist, showing who sang what and in what key.

The only thing we didn't have was a singer, but we kept on practising with Chris and me sharing the vocals and found that we could manage. We also got on well together with no additional personalities to worry about. It's rather strange that we kept the same name Ten Feet Five with just three of us, but we knew that if we kept the name we could ride on our past success when getting gigs, rather than being called Six Feet Three or some other made up name. Life again was beginning to pick up, with my spare time being taken up with practising and playing in the band, but my shitty day job was still there.

Route 66.   A.   Ch P.
Green Onions ✓   G.   Ch P.
Dimples ✓   G   Ch P.
Susie Q ✓   P   Ch P.
Ain't Superstitious ✓ D   Ch P
Round & Round ✓ A.   Ch P.
Memphis ✓   Dk   Pete.
Under the Boardwalk   P   Pete.
Roll over Beethoven ✓   C   Pete.
Talking 'Bout You.   C.   Pete.
In the Moonlight
Sweet Little 16.
If you don't come back.   C   CB.
think it over.   A   CB
that'll be the day.   A   CB
My Babe   D.   CB.
Down Home Girl ✓   G   CB
Down the Road Apiece   A.
Little Queenie.
Reeling & Rocking
Hoochie Coochie Man.
It's so easy.
Mona

When I met Tony and his wife for a drink in 2014, he gave me our old playlist

However, even that was about to change. I was working on my machine one day when the maintenance manager came up to me and said, "I believe you're an electrician." I said yes and he said, "We could do with an electrician in the maintenance department. Would you be interested?" Just the thought of getting away from that machine and back to my old trade meant I immediately said yes before he had time to say anything else. And within a week I was working in the maintenance department. I worked in the factory, and in the houses that Enham Industry owned; this was virtually the whole of the village. This turned out to be the best job I've ever had. I was even told to go ahead and order all the tools and meters I required to do the job. Being the electrician, electrical work was all I was required to do and sometimes there was hardly anything to keep me busy, but with a meter over my shoulder, and screwdrivers in my hand, I could just walk around pretending I was working. This was the job I dreamt of having all those years ago when I was working at the butcher's. Even if nothing happened with the group now I had a job I loved and would quite happily settle for that.

So far I have not mentioned a great deal about my family, especially my brother and sister, mainly because they didn't play a significant part in this period of my life, but also because I don't want to disrespect their memories, which sometimes I think I'm doing. This is not my intention; I only want to give you a full picture of what my life was like. So rather than going into big long story I have written a brief outline about them.

My sister Shirley was a very pretty girl but, unfortunately, she had a very sad life. Until she reached the terrible teens, things were not too bad, but as with most daughters, my dad always worried about her: if she was ever late getting in, he would be out looking for her and that's when the rows would start. Sometimes they were bad: crying, doors slamming and shouting. She often left home to go and live with a friend, only to return home after a falling out, then repeat the scenario at home and then go back to her friend. This would be happening all the time.

One day she asked me if I could give her car a wash and she would pay me; I said okay and gave it a good clean, but when finished, this left me little time to get ready for BB, so I asked her for a lift to Moore Hall and she replied, "I'm not your bloody chauffeur." I thought that was not very nice and wondered why she was so nasty. We later discovered the reason for all the aggression and mood swings; sadly, she was suffering with schizophrenia.

She spent quite a lot of time in Park Prewitt, a mental hospital in Basingstoke, but also periods at home, which sometimes were very difficult for us, when suddenly she'd flare into a rage and we would need to call the ambulance or the police. However, she did eventually marry a patient at Park Prewitt, though thankfully they did not have any children. When her husband died she spent most of her time in her flat drinking tea, smoking cigarettes and collecting religious memorabilia. Sadly, because of her smoking she was diagnosed with cancer and died six months later. It seems so unfair because when she was young, she was pretty and had a good sense of humour and loved going out dancing. Schizophrenia ruined her life and made life for us very unsettling and embarrassing at times. I have great sympathy for people who live with mental illness in the family, for the problems it can bring and the social stigma.

My brother Gerald was eighteen months older than me and had quite a steady life really. Although he had many nice girlfriends he did not want to get married. After leaving school he trained to be a mechanic and stayed in that trade for the rest of his life. Although he didn't marry, he did like children, especially my daughter Lydia, and his face would light up whenever he saw her. I don't know if it was the upheaval at home with Shirley or the thought of responsibility, or if he left it too late, but he stayed a bachelor; in fact he never left home completely. He slept at his partner's house, then called into Mum's in the morning on his way to work to pick up his sandwiches, then after work he would call into Mum's again, have a wash and change, have a cooked dinner then back over to his partner's house for the evening; that was his daily routine, apart from the weekend.

Gerald and I were never really close. I think maybe he begrudged having to look after me when I was young. If I didn't have anybody to play with, Mum would say, "Take your brother with you and look after him." I don't think he liked that very much.

Gerald's main loves were Elvis Presley, drinking and having a smoke. Once we thought he had a problem with the drink as one morning about 2am Mum found Gerald flat out on the settee, with what she thought was blood coming from his mouth. He had for many years been complaining about stomach pains and she feared the worst, so she went down the road to the telephone box and rang the doctor. When he arrived he lifted Gerald's eyelid, turned to my mother and stated "The man's drunk." When she told me this, I don't know how I stopped myself laughing, but knowing the embarrassment and shame she must have felt I put up a good show of looking amazed and shocked. It turned out that he had been drinking rum and blackcurrant all night.

As Gerald got older he gave up being a full-time mechanic and became an HGV driver, which was a good move really because it stopped him from drinking too much. But he did not give up his love for cigarettes or Elvis. Unfortunately, he eventually died of lung cancer. His funeral was very touching as they played one of his favourite songs 'Amazing Grace' over the speaker system in the crematorium and my son Leo played the guitar to it. I don't know to this day how Leo did it sitting next to the coffin and playing the guitar, with his hands shaking so much. The other significant thing that happened that day was my half-brother Keith approached me and asked "Is that right you're my brother?" I said yes but didn't think it was the right time or place to discuss such a delicate subject. Although I didn't see a lot of Gerald he was very generous to Lydia, Leo and myself in his will. As I look at his photos I feel quite sad that when he retired, all he wanted to do was to spend his time going fishing, but unfortunately, he never quite reached that age.

My sister Shirley aged 18

Gerald and I on my wedding day

Looking back on my brother and sister's lives my throat goes tight and my eyes fill up asking myself why their lives were not as blessed as mine. I can't think of any sensible explanation for why this should be, though I still have a sense of guilt, but also gratitude for the way things have turned out for me; and of course, I still have Keith, my half-brother, who I have started to see a lot more. Chris, Tony and I played together for about four or five months and Tony recalls the time we talked about turning professional. I can't remember this, but I'm sure it must have happened. I certainly didn't want to give up my job, the job I'd always wanted. Tony said he'd been professional for many years and his then girlfriend wanted him to give up playing. The writing was on the wall again for another period of uncertainty.

CHAPTER 11

Tony did leave the group and it was left to Chris and myself to break the news to Lance that once again we were on the lookout for a drummer, or anybody else our age who wanted to play in a group. Our problem was in the late 60s most people we knew who had played in bands were either married, planning to get married, or had had their fun in bands and didn't want any more of the hassle with practising, travelling and the late nights. The prospects of finding replacements were not looking too good, and as always you had the extra problem of different personalities and playing music everybody would be happy with.

We didn't know at the time that The Troggs, our friendly rivals, were also having the same problems with their band. Howard (Ginger) Mansfield left The Troggs because he didn't trust Stan or Larry Page, so this left their group trying to find another lead guitarist. This seemed to be an impossible task that caused frustration in the group and led to Dave Wright leaving as well. This left Reg Ball, the bass player, and Ronnie Bullis, the drummer, in the same predicament as us, with a van load of equipment and the remnants of a once very popular band.

After an early guarded relationship, Stan Phillips and Lance decided to work together, both being businessmen and wanting to see a return on their investment from The Troggs for Stan and The Ten Feet Five for Lance. I do not know when, but it was decided that it would be a good idea if Reg and Ronnie joined Chris and me to form another group. We could use The Troggs' name as it was already on Ronnie's drum kit, and use our equipment and van, as neither Reg nor Ronnie could drive. The other problem was Reg and I were both bass players, but as I'd been playing the bass longer

Reg agreed that I should carry on and he would play the tambourine and do the singing.

Our initial practices took place at Stan's workshop for his shop fitting business at Shepherd's Spring. This was a very large building with workbenches, machinery and an assortment of counters and gondolas. Being February, it was very cold, but I did manage to find a way to override the time switch for the hot air system to give us some heating; plus, there was a free vending machine with coffee or hot soup, so we were quite well-equipped to be able to practise.

We started running over the old songs we knew from our previous groups. Ronnie did 'Jaguar and the Thunderbird', Reg 'Dimples', I would do 'Mona' and Chris 'Little Queenie'. I think we all found it a bit strange at first that once we were rivals but now playing together, but the atmosphere was good because we were just happy to be in a band again. There was a very positive feeling about what we wanted to achieve, and furthermore we had two managers working on our behalf who wanted us to succeed, not only for their own kudos in Andover, but also to reward us for staying loyal to them when all the others had left. After many cold evenings at Shepherd's Spring, on the 26th December 1965, we did our first gig at Moore Hall (remember, my nursery/ BB Hall). Although the pop scene in Andover had virtually run its course Lance did find sufficient bookings in Southampton, Camberley and Newbury to keep us going.

One gig I remember vividly during that period before our big break was Calcote Hotel near Newbury. This was a staff party for Van Mopees the diamond merchants. It was an unusual gig because there was no stage, so we played on the dance floor. Usually I don't like this and prefer to be completely separated from the crowd, but this time it worked out very well. As the party progressed the girls got more drunk and started to dance very close to us, so much so that in the end we were playing and dancing with them at the same time. It was a great evening, although the best was yet to come. Reg and Ronnie both worked in the construction industry and in winter when the weather was really bad there were times when there was no work. This was not so bad for me as an electrician,

WILD THING

since not all my work was on building sites, but Reg was a bricklayer and Ronnie was a carpenter so they relied on the building site work; they were both married and Ronnie had young children so this could be a difficult time of year.

I remember Ronnie once telling me things were so bad that once his family had porridge for Sunday lunch; at the time we laughed about it, but now, in retrospect, it was quite hard for them. At the end of the evening Van Mopees were so pleased with the way the evening went they told us we could have any food or drink that was left over. I don't think Ronnie could believe his eyes when he saw what was left over: salmon, every type of sandwich you can think of, cakes, sausage rolls, mince pies and champagne just there for the taking. We all thought it would be nice to have a sandwich and piece a cake and a drink before we packed up, but Ronnie's sense of self-preservation kicked in as he filled his drum cases with everything he could fit in. Not a thought was given to how we were going to pack the drums back in the van. I wonder if he said to himself 'it won't be fu..ing Quaker Oats for lunch tomorrow'? We eventually managed to get everything safely in the van and started our journey home, popping champagne corks and laughing as we drank out of the bottles, whilst feasting off Ronnie's vast food store in his drum cases.

We carried on rehearsing sometimes at Stan's yard, but also at Grately village hall. One practice night Reg said he had a couple of songs in his head that we could try. One was called 'Lost Girl' and the other was 'The Yeller In Me.' We worked on these two numbers and included them in our act.

In the meantime Stan and Lance were still hoping for big things for us, but realised that Andover was not the best place to be to promote a group. London, Liverpool or Manchester were the places to be.

Stan had had previous dealings with Larry Page, The Kinks' ex-manager, through Dave Wright and Ginger, and decided to contact him again, explaining that The Troggs had a new line up and asking if he would be prepared to hear them again. He agreed and arranged for us to meet him and play a couple of numbers. I think the numbers must have been 'Lost Girl' and 'The Yeller In Me,' although I can't be sure. I don't know if Larry was over impressed with us or maybe he was just looking for another group to replace The Kinks, but he said he would like to record us with the view to a record/management contract. Reg and Ronnie seemed to be more excited than Chris and me about having a record released, as we had already had one, only to experience the damage a failed release can have on the morale of a group, even to the point of destruction.

Chris and I were contracted to Lance and Ronnie and Reg were contracted to Stan, so to have another manager would mean that we would be giving away quite a large percentage (I think I'm sounding a bit like Ginger), but not knowing the full details of any contract, or being able to see into the future, I felt it was best just to go along with things knowing I always had my 'screwdriver and meter' job to go back to.

It wasn't long after returning to Andover that Larry contacted Stan saying that he had booked Regent Sound in London for us to record 'Lost Girl' and 'The Yeller In Me.' After making excuses to our employers as to why we couldn't be in work the next day we journeyed to London and Regent Sound.

The only definite thing that I can remember about the recording was that Larry kept saying, "Put some feeling into it." This was a very important lesson we learnt about recording, as it was just as important to put feeling into your playing as playing the right notes or chords; this was embedded in our minds whenever we went into a recording studio. After the session, we returned to Andover and were back to work the next day; then it was a just matter of waiting to hear when, or if, it was going to be released. We eventually heard via Stan that the record was going to be released in February on the CBS label. This was something exciting to look forward to.

Having Larry in London with all his contacts, starting up his new record company Page One Records with Dick James, the Beatles' music publisher, we were more optimistic about getting the airplays required to stand any chance of getting in the charts.

Sadly, after the record's release there were just a few plays on Radio Luxembourg, and without the BBC taking it up, the chances of getting in the charts were very remote. Even with Larry, Dick James and lots of wishful thinking, nothing became of The Troggs' first release. Strangely this did not affect the morale of the group, maybe because we thought we were moving in the right direction; we had two managers in Andover, and Larry Page in London. Again, as with the Ten Feet Five, we could now say on the bill posters 'The Troggs CBS recording artists' and command a few more quid for our gigs.

CHAPTER 12

In 1965, Sybil Burton, Richard Burton's wife, opened a new discotheque in Manhattan called Arthur. The lead singer of the resident group, The Wild Ones, was Jordan Christopher from Ohio, who was a singer/guitarist and had previously been in a group called The Fascinations. Before long, Sybil, 36, and Jordan, 25, were dating, even though she was 11 years his senior, and they eventually got married in 1966. Because of the publicity Sybil received, there was great interest in Arthur and The Wild Ones. This enabled them to get a recording contract with United Artists, but after the release of an album Jordan left the band to seek an acting career.

The Wild Ones carried on with their producer Gerry Granahan, who contacted James Wesley Voight, aka Chip Taylor, brother of Jon Voight and uncle of Angelina Jolie, asking if he could come up with a song for the group as he was not happy with the material they had. Chip Taylor was at the time a house writer for April Blackwood Music. He went into the studio and started strumming some basic chords and adding some sexy words, and he came up with the basic demo called 'Wild Thing' that was given to Gerry Granahan for The Wild Ones. 'Wild Thing' was released on 1 November 1965, but failed to get in the charts. By then Jordan Christopher was no longer in the band and guitarist Chuck Alden took the lead vocal. Chuck later confessed he was never very happy with his performance as he sounded quite nasal.

Although disappointed with 'Lost Girl' not making the charts, we were not devastated, as we had so many people working on our behalf, and were confident we'd have another bite of the cherry later.

In 1965 Larry Page and Dick James formed a record company, Page One Records, in London. Working for them was Colin Frechter, one time record plugger and arranger, who became musical director for Page One. Colin told me that when Page One first started all they had in the office was a phone and no furniture. Eventually, they had the large desk that Larry used. Not long after setting up the company Larry and Colin went to America to meet Chip Taylor, who Larry knew. They told him they had signed a group called The Troggs and asked if he had a song that they could use. After their return from America a demo came over from Goldstar Studios of 'Wild Thing.' They both liked it and thought it would be suitable (if a little off the wall) for The Troggs.

Colin thought that the pipe solo was an ocarina. Apparently, it turned out it had been done by the sound engineer blowing into cupped hands.

The demo was sent down to Andover for us to rehearse along with a song by The Loving Spoonful, 'Did You Ever Have To Make Up Your Mind,' which was a hit in America. Larry thought we could release it here ahead of The Loving Spoonful and, maybe, get in the charts first.

We thought 'Wild Thing' was a much easier number to do so we decided to do that first. After setting up our gear in Stan's workshop we started to mess around with it.

After listening to the demo, which had just three chords, A D and E, we thought that if we didn't heed Larry's words, and do it with feeling, it would be nothing. We knew we needed an opening that would attract attention, so Chris worked out that by bending a string played through a distortion unit this would give us just the right opening. Also, the count in for the first chord, which we laid down with much gusto, was accompanied by Reg shouting "Hit the fucking things Ronnie," and Ronnie shouting back "I am hitting the fucking things"; then hitting them even harder.

From a talking song with a strumming acoustic guitar, we converted it into a hard-hitting, sexy number. I never knew The Wild Ones' version, but have since listened to it. I think they had moved too far away from the simplicity of Chip Taylor's demo. I don't believe any other group could have been as successful with

'Wild Thing' as we were. Many bands, like The Wild Ones, have tried to add extra things in and have killed the simplicity of the number.

Personally, I didn't like the demo when I first heard it; but when it was finished, after we'd introduced many different moods - heavy chords, sexy voice and the mystic ocarina - we really enjoyed playing it. We were still buzzing from 'Wild Thing' when Reg said he had a song that perhaps we could work on, called 'With A Girl Like You.' He had the words and tune, and it sounded more upbeat than The Loving Spoonful's number and it seemed a better choice to follow 'Wild Thing.' I can't exactly remember when we finished working on it, but those were the two songs we ended up recording. Reg then contacted Larry saying we had rehearsed the numbers and were ready. Larry had a session booked for his Page One orchestra at the Olympic Studios in Carlton Street and said he could fit us in at the end of his session.

We duly arrived at the studios one cold February afternoon and waited outside until we were called. We were told we had an hour to get our stuff set up and get the numbers down. We dragged our amps and instruments out of the van and into the studio and were amazed at its size as it was capable of accommodating a full symphony orchestra. The ceilings were very high and the glass window of the control room looked down on us. This was just the studio we needed: we could turn up our volume full blast and really get the feel of it just as we did in Stan's workshop. We must have looked quite small, just the four of us, in this big studio, especially following the full orchestra.

When recording we always used headphones so we could hear everything. Reg used a separate soundproof booth with a glass window so we could all see each other. Colin Frechter recalls about a half an hour before the session started Larry told him to go buy an ocarina. He trawled up and down Charing Cross Road looking without success. Eventually he stumbled across a tiny music shop, near Leicester Square, that sold musical stands, guitar strings and metronomes and he asked if they sold ocarinas. The lady enquired, "What key would you like young man?" He had no idea what key The Troggs were playing 'Wild Thing' in, so he bought one in C.

He returned to the studio and missed the orchestra session but arrived just in time for The Troggs' bit. We recorded 'Wild Thing' and 'With A Girl Like You' in three quarters of an hour. Larry said to Colin, "Okay clever dick, you bought the ocarina so you better play it." He managed to work out the four notes that he would need for a solo; he also knew that he would probably only get one chance to play it as Larry had threatened to put a guitar solo in. It was done with the first attempt and then 'Wild Thing' was complete. Next was 'With A Girl Like You', which was done in two takes. All that remained was for Larry and the engineer to mix the two numbers.

Met up with Colin Frechter in 2016 for the first time in 47 years

We didn't realise at the time just what that three quarters of an hour of recording had achieved. 'Wild Thing' went on to be number one in America and 'With A Girl Like You' took the number one spot in the UK at the same time.

WILD THING

AMERICAN TOP TWENTY

(1) WILD THING............................Troggs, Atco/Fontana
1 (3) LIL' RED RIDING HOOD
                    Sam the Sham and the Pharaohs, MGM
3 (7) SUMMER IN THE CITY......Lovin' Spoonful, Kama Sutra
4 (4) PIED PIPER........................Crispian St. Peters, Jamie
5 (11) THEY'RE COMING TO TAKE ME AWAY HA-HA
                    Napoleon XIV, Warner Bros.
6 (5) I SAW HER AGAIN.........Mamas and the Papas, Dunhill
7 (2) HANKY PANKY..........Tommy James and the Shondells,
                    Roulette
8 (8) SWEET PEA.............................Tommy Roe, ABC
9 (9) MOTHER'S LITTLE HELPER...Rolling Stones, London
10 (10) SOMEWHERE MY LOVE..Ray Conniff & Singers, Columbia
11 (14) SUNNY.............................Bobby Hebb, Philips
12 (6) HUNGRY..........Paul Revere and the Raiders, Columbia
13 (16) THIS DOOR SWINGS BOTH WAYS
                    Herman's Hermits, MGM
14 (17) OVER, UNDER, SIDEWAYS, DOWN......Yardbirds,
                    Epic
15 (30) SEE YOU IN SEPTEMBER......Happenings, B. T. Puppy
16 (26) I COULDN'T LIVE WITHOUT YOUR LOVE
                    Petula Clark, Warner Bros.
17 (23) SWEET DREAMS...................Tommy McLain, MSL
18 (12) PAPERBACK WRITER.................Beatles, Capitol
19 (18) THE WORK SONG..Herb Alpert & the Tijuana Brass, A&M
20 (20) I WANT YOU.....................Bob Dylan, Columbia

1966 US Chart

Britain's best-selling records—last week's figures in brackets.

1	(4)	WITH A GIRL LIKE YOU—Troggs
2	(1)	OUT OF TIME—Chris Farlowe
3	(2)	BLACK IS BLACK—Los Bravos
4	(5)	THE MORE I SEE YOU—Chris Montez
5	(7)	LOVE LETTERS—Elvis Presley
6	(3)	GET AWAY—Georgie Fame
7	(9)	GOIN' BACK—Dusty Springfield
8	(25)	GOD ONLY KNOWS—Beach Boys
9	(14)	MAMA—Dave Berry
10	(16)	VISIONS—Cliff Richard
11	(8)	I COULDN'T LIVE WITHOUT YOUR LOVE —Petula Clark
12	(6)	SUNNY AFTERNOON—Kinks
13	(18)	SUMMER IN THE CITY—Lovin' Spoonful
14	(10)	NOBODY NEEDS YOUR LOVE—Gene Pitney
15	(11)	RIVER DEEP—MOUNTAIN HIGH— Ike and Tina Turner
16	(20)	HI-LILI HI-LO—Alan Price Set
17	(12)	BUS STOP—Hollies
18	(15)	YOU DON'T HAVE TO TELL ME—

1966 UK Chart

At the end of the recording we packed up our gear and Larry told us he'd be in touch when he had some news, so we drove back to Andover. Reg and Ronnie went back to the cold building site. I went back to my meter and screwdriver and Chris continued with his lithographic printing job.

After a while we heard from Larry telling us that Fontana was willing to release 'Wild Thing' which was great news, but we knew from past experiences that getting the BBC to play it would be the most important factor for the record to succeed.

Colin Frechter recalls he was given the job of trying to get plays on the radio. He knew Brian Willie from his days as a song plugger. He used to produce 'Saturday Club' on the BBC and Colin took the record to him and he said they found it interesting and a 'bit off the wall'. He played it on his radio programme and the next thing we knew it had entered the charts at number 38 and then went to number 3. The rest is history...

Back in Andover I started to hear it more on the radio. This was a very strange and exciting experience, and every week I bought the 'Melody Maker' and the 'New Musical Express' to see if it was in the charts. I eventually saw that it entered the charts at 38. Seeing our record in the charts for the very first time was like a dream come true.

Things got even more exciting when we were asked to do 'Thank Your Lucky Stars'. This was a television pop show that went out nationally on Thursday. It was filmed in the Ashton Studios in Birmingham and presented by Keith Fordyce, Brian Matthews and Jim Dale. We were all still working and had to take a day off. I felt quite smug telling my boss, "I won't be in tomorrow; I've got to do a television show."

It was a long drive to Birmingham in a van in the 60s, as most of the motorways and bypasses were not completed and it was always badly congested in the towns. When we eventually arrived at the studio, we were informed that all we needed were the drums and guitars and to take them through to the set then go for a coffee and wait to be called. After a while a girl holding a clipboard came to us and said, "We're ready for you now," so we made our way to the set where Ronnie had set up his drums. We were then instructed, by the voice from the control room, where to stand. After several run throughs, we went to make-up. Seeing each other with make-up on for the first time started the usual group banter, like, "What are you doing tonight love?" This was our first experience of doing television, but the start of many more to come.

To our amazement 'Wild Thing' went from strength to strength and was soon in the top ten. We were still at work. I remember changing a light switch in somebody's house in Enham and hearing the DJ on the radio say, "Here at number 8 with 'Wild Thing' - The Troggs." Reg heard the same programme while on the building site, so that evening we had a meeting and decided to ring Larry to ask if we should pack in our jobs. Realising that we would soon have to start doing more television and interviews to promote the record, he agreed. So, the next day we all gave notice to our employers; Reg, being self-employed, just threw his trowel down and told his workmates he was off and they could share his tools out amongst themselves.

Not all our practising was done at Shepherd's Spring; another place we used was Grately village hall. The caretaker there was always very good to us, and never complained about the noise; in fact he would invite us into his bungalow after practice for coffee. When 'Wild Thing' entered the charts we thanked him by doing a gig at the village hall. It was packed solid, and was the first time we experienced girls screaming at us.

When 'Wild Thing' was in the top ten things really started to move very quickly. Larry started to arrange press interviews and radio and television shows, but he was also working out the type of group he would be able to sell. Four country lads sounding like oiks didn't fit the image he would be comfortable with. Keith Althem, a friend of Larry's who worked for the 'New Musical Express', suggested that some of our names didn't have quite the sound of pop stars and needed to change: Reg Ball to Reg Presley and Ronnie Bullis to Ronnie Bond. Chris Britton sounded okay and they must have thought changing my name to somebody famous would look a little bit suspicious, so fortunately I was left as Pete Staples. With our names sorted out I suppose the next step was how we were going to look on camera.

While Larry was reading an article in the 'News of the World' one Sunday about a boutique in Carnaby Street promoting the latest fashions, he saw a particular product that caught his eye. It looked like white suits with stripes; like deck chairs. He contacted the owner, Sid Brent, and devised a publicity stunt that could benefit The Troggs and his shop, Take 6. The stunt would read that Sid had met The Troggs in his shop a few months earlier and bet them a thousand pounds that they would never get a record in the top five, but now with 'Wild Thing' in the top five he would have to pay up and give them a £1000 worth of gear from the shop. What we actually received were the striped suits, which turned out to be cream with blue and yellow stripes, as well as a couple of pairs of trousers, shirts and jumpers. Sid was very happy with the publicity that appeared in all the top music papers, and we were also happy with our new wardrobe of the latest mod fashions, and our set of deck chair coloured stage suits. Those striped suits became our stage image for a long time, and even today people still say, "I remember those striped suits you wore."

After days of interviews, photo sessions, TV and radio, we realised that we will soon need to start gigging, so with an advancement on our royalties we purchased a new Commer van and a Humber Super Snipe car and employed two roadies, one to drive the van and set up the equipment, the other to drive us around.

CHAPTER 13

Alex King was medium height, slim built, dark haired, smartly dressed and quietly spoken. He was the road manager for the Kinks for a while, but left because of the stress he was under with Ray and Dave fighting and arguing so much. He would be our road manager/chauffeur, driving us around, organising the hotels and generally looking after us.

When we started gigging it was seven days a week of travelling, hotels, playing, interviews, recording, smoking, drinking and motorway cafes - this was no 9 to 5 and go to church on Sunday job. It was very hard, especially for our two roadies driving all over the country and setting up the gear night after night. As I mentioned, travelling in the late 60s was more difficult than it is today, with the lack of motorways and dual carriageways, and we spent many hours cramped up in the car, smoking. Although our agent tried as much as possible to get bookings within reasonable distances of each other, there were times when we could drive to Scotland one day then drive all the way down to Cornwall the next.

Arriving at your hotel after a long drive and being able to have a coffee, stretch out on the bed and watch the TV was lovely feeling, even though on the rare occasion you could end up having to share a room. Reg and Ronnie would sometimes share and sometimes Chris and I would share.

I remember sharing a room with Alex Hosford our van driver, and it was quite a strange experience. He told me he was into yoga and astral travelling. I knew what yoga was but not astral travel. He told me that while lying in bed he could transport himself to somewhere else in the world. My mind pictured him floating up off his bed and disappearing through the ceiling. I listened to all the places he had travelled to without his body, trying to sound interested but thinking, what a load of old crap. But Alex worked so hard that perhaps he did find some enjoyment mentally visiting all these places, and taking his mind away from his very arduous job. Whilst laying there and nearly dozing off, I heard him say, "I think I'll go to China tonight." I couldn't hold it back any longer and said, "You better be back in the morning - we got a gig in Bolton," then I floated off on my own trip and thoughts; relaxation at last.

On another occasion Reg and Ronnie had to share a bed. In the morning at breakfast Reg told us how he awoke in the night but was still half asleep, only to find Ronnie on top of him, getting quite amorous. Ronnie was still asleep and must have been having a lovely dream and thinking he was back at home. Reg said it took all his efforts to get him off.

Ronnie was one of the loveliest blokes you could meet. But in the mornings he was evil. You never spoke to Ronnie until he had had a cup of coffee and something to eat and then you had to be very cautious. After Reg told the story we waited for Ronnie's reaction, which was "You fucking liar," but Reg insisted it was true, and we all realised that we could not mention it again until the coffee had worked its magic. This didn't take too long, and soon we were all able to laugh about it; but I don't think they ever shared a double bed again after that.

Our second release 'With A Girl Like You' was soon climbing the charts and eventually ended up at number one. We were also amazed to be told that 'Wild Thing' had reached number one in America at the same time. This was quite an achievement when you consider we recorded both numbers in three quarters of an hour, whilst having a day off work.

In America 'Wild Thing' was released by two companies, Atco and Mercury. Not knowing anything about the record business we thought this would be a good thing, having two companies releasing and plugging it at the same time, but this turned out not to be the case.

Apparently, Larry had given a master copy of 'Wild Thing' and 'With A Girl Like You' to Sonny and Cher's managers, Charlie Green and Brian Stone. Unbeknown to him they went off and negotiated a deal with Atco for its release. Meanwhile, Larry was also in negotiation with Mercury for it to be released on their label. It was not until 'Wild Thing' was climbing the charts they noticed Atco's release suddenly appear. I don't know if it had ever happened before that two different record companies had both claimed the number one spot with the same record simultaneously.

The problem was that Larry had a contract with Mercury, but not Atco, so the distribution of royalties and who had what became very complicated. Charlie Green and Brian Stone said they had a verbal agreement with Larry to release the record, but I don't think that would have stood up in court as everything in the music industry is done strictly by written contract. It wasn't until years later we found out that Atco settled out of court, but with attorney fees and all the other expenses you get in an American law case, I don't think there was very much left for us. We certainly never felt any benefit from our number one in America. To make matters worse, 'With A Girl Like You', which was going to be our next release in America, was on the B-side of Atco's release. Also, in their haste to get it out quickly they credited Reg as being the writer of 'Wild Thing'.

Larry Page had made one of the biggest cock-ups of all time and unfortunately it was us that dipped out career wise and financially; to what extent we will never really know.

We were kept very busy touring, recording, and promoting and never thought about the money side of things. Dick James suggested we form ourselves into a limited company and we were named as directors along with Dick James' accountant Charles Silver who would look after the company for us. We had a situation whereby Dick James and Larry Page were our managers, record company and music publishers and they also employed somebody to act as our booking agent. We were told that having everything in the one building would be better for us and would enable us to be better informed, as all the answers would all be in the one building. Not knowing all the devious ways of business, we thought it sounded a sensible idea. But later we realised that it wasn't such a good idea, because we didn't have any control over our earnings, or any way of finding out if we were being paid the right amount. We were working very long hours and drawing £35 a week from our company Troggs Ltd. We could have earned more on the building site. This was an unsatisfactory situation, and later did cause a lot of problems within the group. Stan Phillips, being a businessman, must have had his suspicions, as he referred to Larry Page and Dick James as "Hookum and Crookum."

The first half of 66 was taken up by various tours, recording sessions and publicity. Larry employed the services of David Caldwell to be our publicist. David was very good, and arranged many stunts and scoops for us. One of the most memorable was in May 1966 when Muhammad Ali was in London to fight Henry Cooper for the world heavyweight boxing championship to be held at Highbury, Arsenal's football ground. Somehow David managed to arrange for us to meet him when he was training at the White City gymnasium. This made all the national newspapers with photographs of him holding up Chris's hair and another squaring up to us. On 26th May Ali went on to beat Henry in the sixth round on a TKN (technical knockout) due to a terrible cut over his eye. Ali was a great champion and it was an honour to have met him, but I still wished Henry had won.

As I mentioned, we were very busy with gigs all over the place. Looking back through my records I found that in September 1965 I played at the Marine Theatre in Lyme Regis with the Ten Feet Five. This was our last gig before the group broke up. Nine months later in May 1966 I played the same theatre with The Troggs. It was a big difference from getting paid about £40-£60 and then nine months later earning £500-£600 and having girls screaming at you. What a difference a hit record can make.

In 1966 we were voted the Melody maker 'Brightest hope of 1966' and were invited to attend the awards ceremony at the new GPO Tower in London. This was quite an experience for us to get an award and meet Tom Jones, Dusty Springfield, Paul and Ringo, Jimmy Savile, Cathy McGowan and have our awards presented by Johnny Mathis. The tower, which was opened on 8 October 1965, had a revolving restaurant where the awards ceremony took place. It was amazing to be able to stand at the window in the restaurant as it revolved giving you panoramic view of London. The only problem with the revolving restaurant was that you had to make sure if you were standing talking to somebody they were not on the stationary section and you on the moving part, though we did at times finding this amusing and it added a lot of fun to a very memorable day.

In June we did an eight-day tour of Scotland that included the Clan Ball at Glasgow Locarno. This was a wild night as the bouncers tried hard, without luck, to keep the girls off the stage, as bodies, bouncers and mic stands went flying. We were forced back against our amps and speakers. Normally, Reg would move to the front of the stage and tease the girls then get pulled into the crowd - this would add a lot more excitement to the show - but playing in Glasgow that's one thing you would never risk. Although the front part of the stage was mostly occupied by girls, there was always the odd bloke amongst them. While the girls would give you a hug and a kiss, most likely you would get a Gorbals kiss from the fellows: a head-butt. I was lucky that night - I could have lost an eye. Somebody threw a penny and it hit me just above my lip, just missing my eye. When we left the stage, I remember there was no possible way to run across the dance floor as the crowd was so dense, so we frantically crawled on the heads of the fans until we reached the door that led to our dressing room, where we were bundled through by the bouncers.

The night of the Clan Ball, Glasgow

CHAPTER 14

Back in 1963, whilst I was still going out with Hilary, Roy Orbison, Brian Poole, The Searchers and Freddie and the Dreamers were due to play at the Gaumont Theatre in Southampton. Roy was one of Hilary's favourite artists, so we decided to go and see him along with John and Vivian. We set off in my Morris 8, knowing that my petrol pump was temperamental and could stop working without prior warning. The electric pump was located under the bonnet by the passenger seat, and when it stopped working, the engine just died, and I would then shout to John "Kick!" and he would kick under the dashboard until we heard the ticking of the pump. Then we would carry on until the next time, praying it wouldn't pack up completely. We eventually arrived and watched a fantastic show.

I was completely mesmerised by the whole occasion: from the time the curtain went up, I was in another world; in fact I was dreaming I was up there playing. For many days after the show I still had that vision of the curtain rising, and hearing the screams of the audience as the artists appeared on stage. Maybe this was the thing that kept me going through a very bad three-year period. I think I was just chasing a dream.

It took three upsetting and unsettling years, with the splitting up with Hilary and the breaking up of the various bands, before my dream came true.

On 1 October 1966 The Troggs started a 33 day nationwide theatre tour with the Walker Bros, and Dave Dee Dozy, Beaky, Mick and Titch, who I will refer to as DDBMT. Unfortunately, we never played at Southampton on that tour, but nonetheless the dream had come true, and I was definitely on that stage when the curtain went up, listening to the screaming of the girls, and was not just in the audience dreaming.

Doing a 33 day tour was quite hard work as there were matinees as well, so the 33 days turned into 66 performances. The whole show travelled on a bus overseen by the tour manager, whose job was to make sure the hotels were booked, everybody got on the coach, and all the equipment made its way to the next venue.

It felt quite strange after bombing around the country doing our own gigs to suddenly find ourselves on a coach with other top artists we'd never met before. Sometimes the routine did get a little monotonous, but with DDBMT, who lived about twenty miles away from us in Salisbury, there was always the familiar feeling that with our similar accents and humour we had a lot in common.

The compere of the show was a comedian, Don Crockett, who was also an impressionist; we got on very well with him and had many laughs together. One night we all decided to go for a Chinese. He told us a funny game he played when eating out with his mates.

Everybody would order their meal using the voice of a famous person without laughing; the first person to laugh had to pay for the evening. I thought this was a brilliant idea as I could impersonate Snozell Durante or Bernie Winters, Ronnie could do James Cagney, Reg could do James Stewart and Don said he would do Oliver Hardy. I don't think Chris could do anybody, so he could sit back and enjoy the entertainment.

When the waiter arrived to take our order we were all amazed to see he was the image of Stan Laurel, standing there smiling with his order pad and pen. Don couldn't believe his eyes as he looked at him, then turned round and smiled at the rest of us. He turned back to the waiter, smiled, flicked his tie like Ollie and said, "A chicken chow mein my good man." He then looked to us as much as to say, "Follow that." By then we had already buried our heads in our menus trying to hide our smiles and the sniggers, but not wanting to pay for the bill we all managed to do our impersonations and it was agreed that after the meal we had all had so much fun we would pay for our own.

The Walker Bros were very popular: they had the looks, good voices and a massive hit with 'The Sun Ain't Gonna Shine Any More'. They were the final act and usually brought the house down. Scott and John were the most predominant members of the group, singing in front, while Gary played the drums behind them. We all got on very well with John and Gary, but Scott never travelled on the bus; he would travel on his own in the back of a car, wearing a blue duffel coat with the hood up and cuddling a large bottle of Vichy water. We all thought he was a bit star struck and up himself, but I have recently been informed by a friend of his that he was not unsociable, just a very shy and reserved person. Whatever the case, you can't ignore the fact that the guy has a fantastic voice.

When the tour was over we didn't know if we'd ever see the other artists again. There was a good chance that we might bump into DDBMT, but not the Walker Bros or Don. Whilst researching for this book I discovered the very sad news that twelve years after our tour Don had died. He had left show business and started up an ice cream business in his home town, then decided to go into the licensing trade. While training at Samuelson's club in Middlesbrough he was taken ill and was found in the cellar. A week later, April 19, 1978, he died of a cerebral haemorrhage at the age of 47. We only knew Don for the 33 days, but the memory of his fun and friendship will live on for ever.

Although we were working most days we did get home sometimes, and it was on those days I envied the other lads who were all married and had someone to go home to. I remember one cold evening driving back to Andover and Reg saying how he was looking forward to getting in a nice warm bed and cuddling up to the missus, and I thought about the fact that I was going back to a cold bed and nobody. But one evening when I got home there was a letter from Hilary congratulating me on our success with the band and saying how pleased she was for me. I was very surprised and decided to give her a call.

Chatting on the phone was very easy and I asked how she was and what she had been doing. She told me that she had got engaged to Richard, but after arranging everything and buying a house she had got cold feet and they split up, which left her very distraught. I did feel a bit sorry for her, but remembering the very miserable period I went through, partly because of her, I was not too sympathetic, even though I still had a lot of feelings for her; albeit somewhat guarded. Although my life was hectic and I was meeting other girls, I did want to see her again and said next time I was home I would give her a call and we could go for a drink. When I returned to the lounge and told Mum, her reply was "You're not going to start that again are you?" I was a bit taken aback by her sharp response, as I was quite happy knowing that just like the others I would have somebody to come home to. I really think Mum was trying to protect me from any future upsets that might arise; also, now that I was a bit of a celebrity and had some money, Hilary might want to enjoy that as well. But if you fall in love, and I do believe I did, you just follow your heart and don't worry what people say or think.

On my next free day I did contact Hilary and asked her out to dinner. As I pulled up in the group's Humber Super Snipe, I thought I looked the goods in my purple Edwardian suit, mauve frilly shirt and mauve buckled shoes, but walking up the stairs I felt a bit apprehensive as I knew her father and mother from the past and wondered how they would receive me after all that had happened. I also hadn't seen Hilary for many years and wondered if she had changed, but when she opened the door, she still looked just as beautiful.

Since it was such a significant evening I should remember where we went and what we talked about, but I can't. I think the evening must have gone well because 48 years, one miscarriage, two children and three grandsons (Charlie, Fergus (Gus) and James) later, we are still together.

CHAPTER 15

My first bass guitar was a Burns Vista Sonic that I bought on the HP. I played that guitar on 'Wild Thing' and all the earlier hits. Chris also used a Burns 12 string on 'Love Is All Around'. As Burns were the manufacturers of guitars and amps, we approached them and suggested that if they supplied us with new amps and cabinets we would promote their products, which they agreed to. They provided a new amp for Chris, a new bass amp for me and a new PA amp, plus all the speaker cabinets, and we were very pleased with our new free gear. Our first live gig on the continent was in Sweden and not knowing the voltage I told Jonah, our roadie, to make sure he checked the voltage before plugging the gear in.

After arriving in Sweden we booked into the hotel then made our way to the venue where Jonah was setting up all the new gear, and it looked great. The tone controls on the amps were always left at the same settings, so it was just a matter of adjusting your volume to the acoustics of the hall. Today you would have a control console at the back of the hall and the roadie would balance the overall sound.

Chris always tuned the guitars to the ocarina. These were made of clay and often got broken in transit so we regularly had to replace them. Since it was not a popular instrument, music shops kept limited supplies and all in different keys, so we would end up buying whatever was available and Chris would tune in the key of the new ocarina.

We would often get a five-minute warning before going on stage, when Alex would say "Right, go." And, to the screams of the audience, we would run on, plug in our guitars, and go straight into 'Lost girl'. This time when we ran out we noticed that there

90

was a funny smell. We had plugged our guitars in, and started to play, when smoke and bangs came from the amps behind us and we lost all sound. All we could do was unplug the guitars and rush back to our changing room. We later found out that Jonah, in his wisdom, decided to change the 240 Volts settings on the amps to a 110 Volts which he believed was the voltage throughout Europe. In fact Sweden used the same voltage as us, 220/240.

The rest of that tour was a nightmare. We had to borrow equipment from bands that were supporting us, usually a semipro local group with cheap amplifiers and PA systems. All our amps had to be flown back to Burns in London to be repaired. Because we were under contract, nobody else could repair them. Thankfully, this was a one-off situation and we never suffered that problem again, and always carried backup amps just in case.

At Eskilstuna museum, Sweden 1966 (The Rademacher Forges, Sweden)
Playing with the magic links.

Although we had trouble with our amplifiers in Sweden the tour was a success. Even using borrowed equipment, the manager of a club in Stockholm commented that it was the first time in four years he had heard girls screaming.

After leaving Sweden we flew to Berlin which turned out to be quite a strange experience. In the 60s with the Berlin Wall dividing the East and the West you flew into the city, down what they called "the corridor" which looked as though you were flying down the main high street with buildings of the East on one side and buildings of the West on the other. The East did look very austere, with dull looking buildings and the old Trabant cars bellowing out grey smoke, as opposed to the West with its Mercedes taxis, modern skyscrapers and flashing neon signs. After booking in at the Berlin Hilton I was surprised when I turned on the radio to find that the only English speaking programme was AFN for American service men and between all the American pop music they were continually reminding them to be careful when using the telephone as there could be spies listening in.

That evening we went to the Eden Playboy club which had a small swimming pool on the dance floor and we watched a troupe of go-go dancers performing their finale. They jumped into the pool and then invited young lads to join them. It was quite a strange sight to see young, well lubricated German boys in formal suits suddenly jumping and diving into the pool. As special guests, we were invited to throw the girls in and we, of course, obliged, and this encouraged more girls, fully clothed, to jump in and enjoy the fun.

The next morning our German record company, Hansa, arranged a photographic session at the Berlin Zoo. Reg, Ronnie and I were all wearing fur coats that blended in very nicely with the other animals even though I was told mine was more like Bud Flanagan's, which encouraged me to walk along singing 'Underneath the Arches.' Chris was more smartly dressed and opted for a three-quarter length camel coloured coat.

Berlin Zoo

Our next gig was at the huge Deutschlander Halle with a seating capacity of 10,000 where we were to perform with Graham Bonney from Basildon, who was originally the lead singer with one of Larry Page's groups The Riot Squad. He was famous for his hit record 'Super Girl', which got to number 19 in the UK charts, but reached number one in Germany and stayed there for six weeks.

93

This made him more popular in Germany than the UK. Graham, backed by the Remo Four, gave a swinging performance to get the show off to a good start. Also on the bill were The Hollies giving their usual polished harmonies to 'A Taste Of Honey,' 'Reach Out, I'll Be There' and their latest hit 'Stop, Stop, Stop'. We were very popular in Germany and after our introduction the crowd started to shout "Eng -land, Eng-land, Tr-oggs, Tr-oggs' as we rushed onto the stage and broke into 'I Can't Control Myself', followed by 'With A Girl Like You', and the fans were going really wild as we finished our set with 'Wild thing'. As the lights went up four girls came running on the stage holding teddy bears with ribbons around their necks and the word Berlin and handed one to each of us; what a lovely finish to a memorable evening.

The next day we decided to have a look at the Berlin Wall and Checkpoint Charlie which was near the wall. There is a museum showing the various means people have tried to get from the East to the West with some horrific consequences. Looking at the wall and the East German security guards with their automatic rifles made feel quite sad as there were so many wanting to get to the West to visit family and friends, but it would be another 22 years before the Wall came down, on October 9th 1989.

As I mentioned, we were very popular in Germany and on December 4th we started a nine day tour. This was the most gruelling nine days we had ever experienced, or ever wanted to experience again. We were touring with another English band but I can't remember their name. As they had spent most of their career working in Germany, they had, to a certain degree, learnt the language, which was very helpful for us in sorting out any problems. When the tour started it was good and didn't feel as though we were spending 12 hours a day travelling. Living with other band members you always had lots to talk about, but when tiredness crept in and the conversation became more of a hindrance than something to be enjoyed, it definitely started to feel more like work rather than a holiday. We seemed to be continually exhausted and spending the best part of the day travelling to a gig, then we would have maybe another 150km to 200 km to do to get to another gig at 11 o'clock that night. We then had to travel overnight sleeping on the bus; I presume this was to save the promoter another hotel bill. After nine days of hotdogs, coffee, whisky, smoking and lack of sleep this did eventually have an effect on our health, particularly on Reg who one night collapsed on stage and then lost his voice. We were so relieved when we did the last gig and returned to the UK. As Reg had lost his voice and with our poor physical shape we had to cancel some television appearances and take some time off to recover. I would never ever like to do another tour like that again no matter what money was on offer.

We were spending so much money in hotels on extra things that we decided we needed to keep a tighter rein on our expenditure. This would need one of us to check all the bills and pay them as necessary, which could take up quite a lot of our valuable leisure time and nobody seemed keen on volunteering for this additional task. Eventually Ronnie said he would.

Everything seemed to be working okay until one morning just as we were getting ready to catch a flight from Germany to the UK, to do the Joe Loss pop show the following day, we noticed that Ronnie had got the flight times wrong and our plane had already left. As you can imagine with Reg and Ronnie there were quite a lot of "Fucks" flying around as Reg told Ronnie how careless he was and that he should have checked it and Ronnie said if Reg could do it better he should do the job. After all the shouting, swearing and incriminating remarks we had to decide what we were going to do. We rang Larry and told him of our predicament and he contacted the BBC to find out what position was.

It was not the answer that we wanted to hear. Apparently, we were the main act and if we let them down we would not get any more bookings from the BBC. This was quite a frightening prospect, as most of the television and radio programmes then were run by the BBC. We checked with the airport but found there were no available seats on any flights going to the UK that day; this started Reg and Ronnie off on another of their verbal battles that never ever seemed to solve anything. Our only option was to try to hire a plane at great expense, or lose any future radio and television with the BBC. We decided that we would have to get back to the

UK at all costs and we frantically rang around to find a private plane that would take us.

We eventually found one company that would be willing to do it for £1300 which we accepted, but we had to explain to them that we didn't have the money in cash, but would draw the money out and pay them when we arrived in the UK. Fortunately, they agreed and we made our way down to the airfield. The plane was a small twin engine six seater and the pilot and co-pilot were not in uniform, just wearing trousers and shirts, but luckily they spoke good English and described the take-off procedure and how long it would take to get to the UK. Although cramped the flight was interesting as we were so close to the pilot and co-pilot that they gave us an ongoing commentary of the procedures they were performing. Eventually we arrived at Gatwick where Reg, having the largest bank account, arranged a bank transfer to pay for our chartered flight. The next day we did the Joe Loss pop show and explained to a very grateful producer the lengths we had gone to not to let them down.

Apart from that, 1966 was a very good year for us and the country. England won the World Cup; if Churchill was alive then, maybe he would say that was our second finest hour. We also had been successful and busy recording and promoting 'Wild Thing', 'With A Girl Like You', 'I Can't Control Myself' and 'Any Way That You Want Me', all of them getting in the charts. We also released one EP, 'Troggs Top No1' and one LP titled 'From Nowhere' that stayed in the charts for 16 weeks, and peaked at number 6. By the end of the year we all feeling very tired, so much so that Alex Hosford our road manager decided he had enough and quit.

Fortunately, Alex King mentioned Peter Jones, who he knew and who also worked for The Kinks and was looking for work. He could be the replacement for Alex Hosford.

Peter, whose nickname was Jonah, told us he worked for The Kinks but found it very stressful with their continual arguing and fighting and one evening whilst driving the van on the M6 from a gig at the Central Pier Marine Ballroom Morecombe he fell asleep and the van careered off the motorway, hitting a stationary lorry.

Also in the van was Pete Quaife, The Kinks bass player, who on this occasion had preferred to travel with Jonah. They were both badly injured and were rushed to Warrington Hospital where Quaife had a broken foot and a cracked skull and Jonah had pelvis and head injuries. After a long spell in hospital, without a visit from Ray or Dave, or a letter of sympathy from the management, he decided that on leaving hospital he would be unable to carry on working for them.

Driving a van or car for a pop group always carries a high risk of accident, due to lack of sleep, boredom or just the amount of time you spend on the road. The Loot experienced a similar accident in 1968 (which I will talk about later). Although we never had an accident, we nearly had a complete disaster when our car caught fire.

There was a short period in 1968 after Alex King had left when we had to drive ourselves to gigs. Chris and I had held full driving licences for many years but Ronnie had only just passed his test and was not 100% competent in all situations. As our Humber Super Snipe was in the garage Stan kindly lent us his Ford Zodiac Mk4 to do a gig up north. On the way home on the M1 we decided to have a break, have a cuppa and use the toilet. After returning to the car, Ronnie asked if he could have a go at driving, and we thought this was a good idea and would give Chris and me a bit more time to rest. I sat next to Ronnie and explained the controls. We set off down the motorway, Ronnie hunched over the steering wheel with a cigarette hanging out of his mouth.

With the heater blowing nicely around my legs, it wasn't too long before my head had dropped on my chest and I was asleep, only suddenly to be woken up by Ronnie shaking my arm asking "What's that red ball following us?" With Reg always looking up at the stars and talking about the solar system and saying "I wonder if there's life out there," I thought perhaps we were about to experience a visitation, but looking at the reflection on the windscreen and noticing a funny smell I soon realised that the reflection was coming from the floor of the car and not from the rear window. I looked down to see a big glowing red ring. It seemed that Ronnie was so focused on the road that his cigarette

97

missed the ashtray, landed on the floor and was burning a hole in the carpet and underfelt. I yelled at him to "Pull over! Pull over!" and we jerked and shuddered on to the hard shoulder.

We all jumped out as the smoke got thicker and we tried to beat it out with our hands, but it was no good, the felt was burning very quickly under the carpet and it wouldn't be long before it would be completely out of control. We needed to find water very quickly, but looking at the surrounding area there was none. The only thing we could do was piss on it. Our problem was, we had only just stopped at the service area and emptied our bladders. In desperation Ronnie said that as he caused the problem he would try to do his bit. He did look quite comical with one leg on the dashboard and one on the passenger seat and he held the steering wheel as he aimed at the now growing red hole. After a good dowsing we were relieved that he had put it out. We did however still have the embarrassing task of returning Stan's car with a big hole in the carpet and a smell of smoke and pee.

Ronnie was the one that that always found himself caught in the most comical predicaments and he gave us lots of laughs. This was very welcome as travelling in the car day after day was very boring and not a lot of fun. Reg was often scathing about Ronnie's misfortune and smugly referred to him as the 'group's pet'. Being in a band you expect a lot of mickey taking; we called it banter. Reg could dish it out but didn't like it directed at him and could turn nasty very quickly if something uncomplimentary was said about him.

Ronnie's funniest misfortune was when we were flying in a BEA Viscount. Halfway through the flight he decided he needed the toilet and made his way to the front of the plane, but as soon as he got to the door the captain made an announcement: "Please extinguish your cigarettes, fasten your seat belts and return to your seats as we will be experiencing some turbulence." Ronnie thought that as he was already at the toilet door he would be very quick and he entered the toilet, closing the door. The plane started to sway, then suddenly drop. Ronnie must have had a difficult time trying to do the necessary and with the turbulence getting progressively worse he had no chance to get back to his seat, as we were thrown all over the place. Suddenly the toilet door opened and Ronnie appeared. While he was still holding the toilet door the plane dropped again, causing Ronnie to fall forward and lift the door completely from its hinges. As the plane dipped and swayed from side to side, Ronnie staggered up and down the aisle, two steps to the right, two to the left, as he continually tried to rehang the door. I was in stitches watching him doing the military two steps as he grimly held onto the door. Being an ex-carpenter he knew all about door hanging and it wasn't too long in between the turbulence that the door was back on its hinges. Making his way back down the aisle to his seat, he was greeted with smiles and congratulations from the passengers for his impromptu on-board entertainment.

CHAPTER 16

Stan lived in a very large cottage in Charlton with his Alsatian dog Digger. Being gay and having a very successful shop fitting business he had the money to make it look beautiful: leather seats, red three-piece suite, oil paintings, antique tables and chairs and a grand piano in the conservatory. It really was a beautiful place, but somewhat a fairyland (I mean that in the nicest way).

Because of our success Stan came into contact with many gay people, some of them perhaps hoping he could help with their musical careers. Needless to say, they were all male and could be found at various times hanging around White Cottage.

When Dave Wright left the original Troggs, I'm sure Stan felt very sorry for him, because he was the one that did all the groundwork enabling us to achieve what we did. Like Ginger, he left The Troggs a couple of months too early, otherwise they both could have had the success we enjoyed. If that had happened Chris could still have been a lithographic camera operator and I could still be at Enham with my screwdriver and meter.

Hoping to ride on our success Stan decided to form another group for Dave, called The Loot. As I mentioned earlier, most of the original groups in Andover had disbanded: The Senators, Ten Feet Five, Redwoods, Strangers and The Just Men had all disappeared, leaving musicians with their hopes of hitting the big time long gone.

With all this dejected talent about Stan had no difficulty in creating another group that he hoped would follow in our footsteps. They were young, good-looking, very good musicians, full of fun and completely wild.

Johnnie Bates was a tall blonde handsome lad and he had sung with The Just Men and had previously released a solo record

'Where Were You Last Night?' Unfortunately, it didn't make the charts. The lead guitarist would be Bruce Turner, ex Emeralds, Senators, and Trendsetters. On bass was Dave Glover ex Redwoods and Ten Feet Five. The drummer was Roger Pope who played in a Southampton group called the Sole Agents and Dave would be the rhythm guitarist.

Stan approached management with The Loot the same way as he did with the original Troggs. He would supply the gear, provide a place for them to rehearse and pay them a wage. Needless to say, White Cottage became a gathering place where all your needs were catered for: food, booze, the use of a car and a bedroom for any girl you wanted to take back. This was an enjoyable existence for the band and practising was fitted in when it was convenient.

I remember calling one day, knocking on the door and finding there was no answer, so I walked in, shouting "Is there anybody at home?" I heard a girl's voice from upstairs call out, "Pete, upstairs." When I reached the landing there were three doors, the bathroom and two bedrooms. "In here Pete," the voice came from Stan's bathroom, "You can come in." So I walked in to see two young girls in the bath. My mouth dropped open as one of them stood up. I got the full frontal. "Pass me the towel," she said, pointing to the heated towel rail, and then the other one stepped out just as I was passing the towel. The first one wiped her front then handed me the towel saying, "Can you dry my back?" After obliging and drying her back and bum the other one wanted the same treatment. I realised I was getting into a bit of an awkward situation. I knew things could have progressed from there if I wanted, but knowing their boyfriends, and that the girls also knew Hilary, I could be in a hell of a lot of trouble if word got out, so I played it cool like it was a bit of fun and an everyday occurrence; which perhaps it was at White Cottage.

When The Trendsetters packed up Bruce said he didn't know what to do. (Oh, I know that feeling.) He approached Larry Page, and asked if he had anything. Larry told him there was a group in Andover that he might sign up, but they needed a lead guitarist. On contacting Stan he was told the boys needed somebody to get things moving as they just seemed to be hanging around the house day and night. The Fiesta Hall was booked for a week and The Loot then rehearsed for eight hours every day until they were ready to leave their comfort zone at White Cottage and go out into the proper world as a pop group. As I mentioned before, in the late 60s, gigs were not easy to come by, so The Loot still had plenty of time on their hands. Some of this was spent in the local pub. One evening while sitting there the conversation turned into farting, and how explosive the gases were. After many jokes about how true it was, they decided to try an experiment. It was agreed that when somebody felt they had built up enough wind they would go out to the toilet, drop their trousers and pants, bend down and with the other person holding a lighter near their arse, they would fart and see what transpired!

After a few pints Dave said he was ready for the experiment and John Bates said he had the lighter, so off they went to the dark cold outside toilet. With trousers and pants down and Batesie ready with the lighter the experiment was about to begin. Would it sound like a motorbike backfiring or a V2 rocket? All that was needed now was the confirmation that the gas was just about to be released. However, unbeknown to the Dave, John heard footsteps entering the toilet so decided to make a quick exit. After passing John on his way out this fellow was confronted with a bare arse stuck up in the air and Dave's voice declaring "Right, I'm ready Batesie."

One afternoon I was at the White Cottage talking to Stan when one of The Loot walked in with a new girl, said hello and took her straight upstairs. A few minutes later we could hear rhythmic banging directly above us. Stan just smiled as he pointed to the ceiling above us and didn't seem to mind they were using his bed. In fact, he found it quite amusing, so I was not shocked to learn that one afternoon just before Christmas a member of The Loot brought a girl back, and as he passed the dining room he took a candle from the candelabra, then took her upstairs to the bedroom. As there was no power cut, I can only assume what the candle was used for.

Stan had many parties, and always dined in style. Christmas dinner was a very grand affair and we were all invited. With the table beautifully laid out with silver cutlery and cut glass, Stan would light the candles, setting the atmosphere fit for the occasion. Two of the candles when lit seemed to join in the festive spirit and were happily glowing creating a magical scene from a Christmas card. But the other one he was having difficulty lighting. Eventually he got it alight, only for it start crackling and spitting like a Roman candle on firework night. Stan stood back, frowned and said, "What's up with this bloody candle?" We all guessed where that candle had been and what it was used for, but we kept our heads down, while trying to hide the smirks on our faces.

Stan eventually managed to get The Loot a recording contract with Larry and released their first record in January 1967, a number taken from our album called 'Baby Come Closer'. He also managed to get them on a tour with us in February with Gene Pitney. The tour was similar to the Walker Bros tour, playing in major towns and cities in England, Scotland and Ireland and started at Finsbury Park on February 7th and ended 28 days later in Coventry. Including the matinees we did 56 shows. On our last tour we had had DDBMT, but this time we had all our mates from Andover: an ex-Senator, ex-Ten Feet Fiver and ex-Trogg, a representative from every group I had played in. Never would I have believed that three years before, when watching Roy Orbison in Southampton and dreaming I was on the stage, that I would be up there and that my mates in Andover would be performing on the same bill.

There was always a lot of fun on this tour. On one occasion we watched The Loot squirt water pistols from the wings at Normie Rowe and The Playboys, a popular act from Australia, as they battled through their set; fortunately they took in good fun and were still friends at the end of the tour. Halfway through there was a bit of a scare when Gene Pitney started to lose his voice. This could have caused big problems for the tour. One morning he said he would have to see a doctor. On his return he informed us that after telling the female doctor his problem, she told him to drop his trousers and pants and bend over and then stuck an injection in his arse making him yell out. Thankfully, to the relief of everybody this did clear up the problem with his throat; also the doctor had a private demonstration on how Gene could hit those high notes. The tour did have some more serious problems. Quite frequently, Reg's mike would stop working; it happened so often that we wondered if it could have been sabotaged by Gene Pitney's crew. It got so bad that one night Reg threw the dead mike on the floor in disgust and walked off, leaving us on stage not knowing what to do, then returned with another mike and apologised to the audience.

When you're on tour with other groups, rather than changing the amps over you often shared equipment. You only played for about half an hour so it was also unnecessary to have extra instruments on stage as backup. There was one night when I wished I had had a spare bass on stage, when halfway through a number one of my strings broke. This had never happened before and my first thought was to find another bass. After charging off the stage in a panic trying to locate another, I aimlessly ran up and down stairs and through corridors trying to locate the dressing rooms. I eventually came across a door and charged in, only to discover it was the boiler room. I was completely lost but could still hear the boys playing somewhere in the distance. I frantically ran up more stairs and corridors eventually finding a dressing room, and I pushed open the door, ran in and shouted "Can I borrow a bass?" There was a complete look of bewilderment on their faces as I just grabbed this bass laying in its case, and ran out the door.

By following the sound coming from the stage, I found it easier finding my way back. With great relief I ran back on stage, plugged in the bass and joined in again. But, unfortunately, I was completely out of tune, as we tuned our instruments to the ocarina and not concert pitch. My borrowed guitar was out of tune with Chris and the first two notes I played sounded terrible; the looks he gave me really showed his feelings. At the end of the number we quickly tuned up and then went on to complete the set. When we got back to the dressing room the air was blue and my name was mud. I had never broken a string on stage before and this was to be a learning curve for us all: after that it was decided in future we would always have backup instruments and amps on stage at live gigs.

The Loot on Gene Pitney tour with us, Putting their stage make up on. From back row l/r Dave Glover, Bruce Turner, John Bates. Front row l/r Roger Pope and Dave Wright

Ireland was one of my favourite places to play. In 1966 we did the Walker Bros tour, playing at the ABC Belfast on 19th October, then the Adelphi in Dublin on the 20th. In 1968 we did the Gene Pitney tour playing the ABC on March 8th and the Adelphi on March 9th. On one of these tours - I can't remember which - we were met at the airport by some students who told us that they were raising funds for the Students' Union and would like, as a prank, to kidnap us and hold us to ransom, hoping the promoter would pay some money for our release. As we thought that this would be a bit of fun and maybe get some publicity we agreed, so we got into their car and were taken to a flat somewhere in the city. They then telephoned the theatre and started their negotiations with the promoter, but he was not prepared to hand over any money and as it was getting nearer the time when we should be at the theatre, they reluctantly let us go without any payment being received. On reflection, this was quite embarrassing, realising that promoter obviously thought more of his money than he did of us performing that night.

The Irish certainly do have a sense of humour as I found out once whilst waiting at the airport in Belfast. I was sitting down enjoying a cup of tea when this scruffy old lady came over to me and said, "Cross my palm with silver, sir, and I will tell your fortune." I really didn't worry about my fortune, but did feel charitable enough to cross her palm with half a crown and she picked up my cup, swished it around, then looked deeply into it; then turning to me she said, "You are going on a journey," put the cup down and walked away. I thought that at least she could have told me I would marry somebody beautiful and have lots of children. But then what did I expect for half a crown?

When visiting Belfast we always stayed at the Drumkeen Hotel in Ormeau Rd. This was a very friendly establishment run by two brothers. In 1992 I was surprised to read in the papers that on 30th December a bomb was placed in the car park at the rear of the hotel, causing extensive damage and blowing out all the windows. Fortunately, in the 60s the troubles had not really started. We did see the odd fire in the street, either a protest or a celebration of some kind, but nothing more sinister than that. Before Northern Ireland and the Irish Republic joined the EU there was always border security guards. Once we were travelling from Northern Ireland on our way to Dublin when we were stopped at the border checkpoint. Jonah, our road manager, had to take every piece of equipment out of the van for them to check; I presume this was for weapons but he was then told to remove the backs of all the speakers, so they could be checked for any concealment. This Jonah was not prepared to do and he told them if they wanted to look they could do it themselves. Realising that this would be a long operation and would hold up the flow of traffic the Garda told him he could put the gear back in the van then stamped our passports and we drove on. On our return journey, late one night, we were beginning to worry about whether we were going to encounter the same problems at the border, but to our amazement when we got there we found the crossing was unmanned and we drove straight through.

Having Irish ancestors I've always felt an affinity with Ireland, and very much at home there. It reminds me of my childhood when children could be seen playing happily in the streets, with the church and your parents strongly dictating the way you should behave. This might have some reflection on why, all the time we played in Ireland, I never received any sexual favours from any girl but I'm sure that somebody out there would try to tell me differently. I must have had some effect on two girls from Belfast as they arrived uninvited in   Andover for my wedding. I was very surprised but flattered to see them and after the church service we invited them to join us at the reception.

CHAPTER 17

1967 started off quite well with 'Give It To Me' reaching number 12 in the charts, and in May 'Night Of The Long Grass' reached number 17. In our complete naivety we assumed everything we released would get into the top twenty. In July, we released 'Hi Hi Hazel' that only made number forty. Concerns started to creep in about our future ability to produce hit songs and our popularity with the record buying public. Another concern was that after five hit records we still didn't seem to have any money, and the people that seemed to be making the money were the songwriters.

This became very contentious when I pointed out to the group that out of our last five releases, Colin and Larry had commandeered four of the B-sides. The writing and arranging of some of these would be finished in the studio by us on the same day of recording. Bearing in mind that the B-side gets the same royalties as the A-side, Reg, Larry and Colin were coining it in. Feeling that Chris, Ronnie and I were not getting a fair share of the royalties I suggested we have a meeting with Larry and tell him our concerns and suggest that it would be fairer if we took it in turns at having the B-side. This was agreed and a meeting was arranged at a restaurant.

After eating I brought up the subject about the fairness of sharing the B-sides, but I think Larry was caught off guard and he went into his usual rhetoric of how he had made us, that he was a director of Page One Records and didn't get record royalties or any money from gigs and that this was no way of thanking him for all that he had done for us. I was quite surprised when Reg suddenly completely changed sides and agreed with him; then Ronnie jumped ship, and Chris, as usual, said a load of nothing, leaving me on my own looking like Mr Troublemaker. After that day I'm sure Larry was very wary of me and I was very wary of my friends' loyalty to the group and each other. My concerns were justified when in 1969 I was treated in the most treacherous way.

After the failure of 'Hi Hi Hazel' we were unable to get any radio or television. This can be quite concerning as you do need to keep in the public eye to keep the gigs coming in. Our publicists David Caldwell and Larry were the masters at publicity stunts. The most memorable, apart from the Muhammad Ali scoop, was Marquis the lion.

The press were told that we were going to record a song called 'The Lion' and needed to record a live lion's roar, and that to do this we had to hire a lion from Mary Chipperfield of Chipperfield's Circus.

The recording studio at the Marquee Club Soho was booked for this stunt and the press duly turned up to see the lion in a recording studio. Watching through the glass window in the safety of the control room we watched Mary bring Marquis the lion in to the studio. He was a big bugger! There was a small stage in the studio and Mary was asked if she could get the lion to stand on the stage and secure his chain so the group and press could go in.

After she had chained him to the stage, we were invited to enter the studio. Mary was very relaxed about the situation, which made us feel confident and not particularly worried. The control room suggested we put some headphones on and open our mouths to make it look as though we were singing, and Mary was asked to get Marquis to open his mouth to make him look as though he was roaring. After the press had taken a few photos, everybody was relaxed and treating it more as a joke. Somebody suggested it would look more realistic if we put a mike in front of him, so the studio engineer produced a microphone and stand and placed it in front of Marquis.

The press happily snapped away, but unknown to us all somebody had plugged the mike in. Marquis, curious about this object in front of him, decided to give it a lick and in return got an electric shock. As he pulled his head back his chain, which was tied to the stage, lifted the stage and rattled a load of metal fittings that were stored underneath; this really frightened him and he went

109

berserk and roared. The press, with wide eyes and mouths open, made a dash for the door. As they were on the floor and we were on the stage they had a head start on us to get out first; by the time I got there they were fighting each other trying to get out, shouting "Get out, get out" and with the lion roaring behind me I was shitting myself. Seeing a grand piano with the lid open, I decided that climbing into that would be my last desperate attempt to save myself if the lion got free. Fortunately, we all eventually got out of the studio and in the corridor we started to laugh about it, more in relief than fun. If Marquis hadn't licked that microphone I don't think the papers would have bothered with our stunt, but as they were so keen to tell their story of how they nearly got mauled to death by a lion we made the nationals.

In the recording studio with Marquis

Although being crammed into a small recording studio with Marquis the lion was quite dangerous, our next stunt also carried a certain amount of risk. The plan was that we would tell the press we were getting a polo team together to challenge Prince Charles to a match. The date was fixed for the stunt and we arrived at the stables where we were fitted out with helmets, shirts, breaches and polo mallets. As none of us could ride and I certainly hated horses, we were hoping just to sit on the horses in full gear and for the press to take photographs. Seeing us trying to get on the ponies, the press soon realised that we didn't had a clue about horses or polo and this was just a publicity stunt. After taking photographs of us in a line, they decided that they would need to see some proper action. A cameraman suggested that if he went to the bottom of the field, and stood on the willow horse jump, we could gallop down with our mallets in the air and he could capture some real action. We agreed to this knowing full well that a gallop was out of the question and was most probably going to be a jog.

After the cameraman had positioned himself on the jump, he shouted, "Let's go," but after kicking the ponies in the ribs several times and saying "Gee up" mine just didn't seem to want to move. I remembered Hilary telling me that when their horses wouldn't go in the horsebox they would slap them on the rear and shout, so I relayed this bit of knowledge to the reporter standing behind me and asked if he would do the honours. The next thing I heard was somebody screaming "Yee hah," followed by a loud slap. My pony's head shot up and he seemed to trot on the spot for a little while before he just took off like it was the start of the Grand National. With the mallet in one hand and the reins in the other, I held on for dear life as he bolted down the field, my helmet sliding sideways over my ear and my shouts of "Stop" no more understood than "Gee up." I approached the waiting cameraman at high speed and as we were heading straight for the willow jump, I thought, "Oh shit - he's going to jump it." My thoughts quickly went into risk assessment mode: do I jump off and hope I don't get trampled on, or do I drop the mallet and hold on tight and pretend I'm Harvey Smith. The decision was soon taken out of my hands as the pony suddenly stopped dead and I found myself flying through the air and landing on my back at the foot of the jump with the wind knocked out of me. I was relieved when I saw the cameraman come running over, but surprised when he said ,"That's great, hold it there," and photographed me prostrate on the ground and gasping for breath. Satisfied that he had enough material he then asked me if I was okay. By then I was able to speak without feeling any severe pain, so I said, "I think I'm okay." Fortunately, none of those photographs were used, but the pictures of the four of us lined up on the ponies were used and did make the nationals.

Whilst we were changing out of our polo gear our publicist asked what we thought about parachuting from a plane as a publicity stunt. The other three, trying to be very macho, said yes, but still nursing my bruises from a six foot fall and thinking what could happen to me from a 10,000 foot fall, I told him to fuck off. I also knew that this would never happen as Reg was afraid of flying.

After I mentioned to Larry about the fairness of sharing the B-sides, things then did start to change. We did take it in turns at having the next B-side, but I was still not happy that after having worldwide hits and continually touring we still had hardly any money in the bank. Chris and Ronnie were of the same opinion. As Reg was earning so much more with his song writing royalties he didn't feel it so much.

Back in Andover, Stan and Lance were also concerned why Larry would never allow us to tour in the USA. Pointing out that having had a number one over there the money we could have made would have been quite considerable, coupled with the cock-up he made with 'Wild Thing' in America, we all agreed Larry was costing us too much money and we would have to take control of our own affairs or we could find ourselves without any money and back on the building site. Stan pointed out that Larry and Dick had complete control over us as they had the management, music publishing and recording contracts; they even had an in house booking agency and an associate of Dick James as our accountant. We had put our trust in Larry and believed him when he told us that if we kept everything under the same roof, the answers to all questions would be readily available rather than traipsing around trying to get information from all over the place. At the time we thought this was a good idea but in retrospect we can see how naïve we were not to think that if he was our manager working on our behalf how could he, as the MD of Penny Farthing records, do the best deal for his record company? He would be negotiating with himself. We did appreciate all that Larry had done for us but we just had to get ourselves out of this tangled web. The only way we could do this was to get our contracts revoked.

The first thing to do was to change our accountants and get a thorough investigation underway on where all the money was going. We gave notice to our existing accountants and informed them that we were placing our accounts with Howell Wade and Co and that our accounts should be forwarded to a Mr Stark of that company. Mr Stark was a corpulent, red faced, old-fashioned schoolteacher type, complete with glasses on the edge of his nose and leather patches on his jacket sleeves. When Mr Stark received our books he informed us that it was very unusual to receive accounts written in pencil and he would have to make an appointment with Page One Records to look at their accounts to clarify the exact money paid to us. After visiting Page One he arranged a meeting with us and informed us that whilst at their office the record company instructed a secretary to walk around with him and write down everything he said. This he found very obstructive and intimidating and had never experienced anything like it before. This confirmed our suspicions that Page One were getting very worried about us asking any questions about the money. So we decided, with the backing of Stan and Lance, that we would instruct solicitors to give notice to Page One that we wished to sever our management and recording contracts with them. This was purely on the basis that our trust in them had completely gone and we felt they were looking after their own interests rather than ours.

CHAPTER 18

Harvey Block Associates were a booking agency which Larry used. When we told them our plans to try and terminate our contracts with Page One they became very interested. They contacted Stan and Lance and told them that they had very good American lawyers and believed they could break our contract with Page One and get us a more lucrative deal in the States, but with our experiences with 'Wild Thing' in the dodgy American music industry we were reluctant to get involved with lawyers unknown to us across the pond.

Derek Block the MD of the company was very understanding about our reluctance to get involved in any new contracts, but assured us all we needed to do was go over there and listen to his attorney; his company would give us return airfares to America and supply accommodation whilst there and all we had to do was just listen to the attorney. We didn't have to sign anything, just listen.

Stan and Lance agreed that no harm would come from going over there and listening and then coming back and deciding what we wanted to do, so we agreed. From that point on it turned out to be a covert operation. Only the wives, Stan and Lance should know our plans. On our arrival at Kennedy airport we were picked up by two record company executives and taken to a big apartment in New York. Our first two days we were taken out in the evenings and wined and dined, and the record company even held a party for us and invited the press who were very eager to talk about us, enquiring why we'd never toured America. It was during one of those interviews that I realised that certain words we use had a different meaning in America. One reporter asked me what my job was before I became famous and I told him my first job was a faggot and sausage maker. With his pen and pad ready to write he looked up at me wide eyed with his mouth open and said, "You made faggots? How did you go about that Pete?" Not realising what a faggot was in America I went on to describe how I used to mix the meat up, put seasoning in, roll it up in little balls then put them in the oven and they were made. After being told what a faggot was in America and seeing the amount of amusement and interest it caused I often retold that story at other interviews.

Another time I fell foul of the language was when I rang down to the reception in a hotel to arrange an early morning call. When I was young and needed to get up early my mum would say, "What time do you want me to knock you up?" This is an old English expression dating back to the times when people didn't have pocket watches or clocks and would pay a "knocker upper" to go round with a long pole and knock on their bedroom window or front door to wake them up. Unaware that that phrase meant something else in America I was rather taken aback with the receptionist when I asked her if she could "knock me up at 7:30 in the morning" and got a very abrupt frosty reply "I beg your pardon sir?" I later found out that "knock you up" in America was getting your leg over.

On day three we had an appointment with Marty Machat, a very well-known entertainments lawyer, who represented Phil Spector, Sam Cooke and the Rolling Stones. We were driven to Manhattan to Marty's office and asked to wait in the reception. When we entered the office we were surprised to see not a man in a suit and tie, but somebody leaning back in his chair with an open neck shirt; he was wearing a shoulder holster, gun and cowboy boots with his feet up on the desk. After inviting us to sit down he ordered coffee and told us about the other groups and artists who had unfair contracts that he'd broken and that he could do the same for us. He'd sign us up with new record company with a big advance and a larger percentage on our sales. We all agreed that it would be great if he could do that, but we would need to discuss it amongst ourselves in private. This he agreed to but said he would want to know very quickly otherwise the deal would be off.

When we got back to our apartment we feared the telephone might be bugged so we decided it would be best to move into a hotel. We thanked our hosts for their hospitality but said we needed to book into a decent hotel so we could discuss Marty's proposal in private. They were not too happy with the idea, but rather than frighten us off they agreed and booked a hotel then ordered us a taxi. They said they would call us the next day and take us back to Marty's so we could sign the contract.

They didn't wait till the morning but contacted us later that day to ask when we would be ready to sign. We informed them we were waiting for Stan to arrive before we made a decision; this did not go down too well and we were threatened that if we didn't sign in the morning the deal was off. We said we would ring back later to let them know our decision. We then had a long heated discussion amongst ourselves about what we should do. I was of the firm opinion we had promised Stan we wouldn't sign and should stand by that, but the others felt that we would never get another chance like this and were willing to sign. Yet again I was on my own, but I could not go back on my word. The boys' attitude gave me concerns about what their word or loyalty meant. A couple of years later I found out to my cost that loyalty meant nothing to them and betrayal took its place.

As soon as we got to the hotel the first thing we did was to ring Stan and tell him the situation. He was adamant that we were not to sign anything as he had taken legal advice and the opinion was that if we signed anything Page One would slap a writ on us as soon as we got back. Being concerned about the amount of pressure being put on us, Stan decided that he would get the next available flight over and was soon winging his way to our aid. He arrived late evening and decided that he would have to get us back to England a bit quick. The first thing he suggested was to change hotels so they couldn't find us; that would give us some breathing space to arrange our escape. We checked out of the hotel and booked into another one a few miles away. After checking in Stan said he was tired and was going to bed and we would talk about it in the morning.

So we all went to our rooms. I was in bed no longer than half an hour when there was a knock at the door, and when I opened it there was Stan standing there in his underpants saying, "They've found out where we are, get dressed, we're checking out." Apparently they found out because we had asked the previous hotel reception to order us a cab, and they were able to find out from the Yellow Cab Company where they had dropped us off. We were determined not to make the same mistake twice and decided to walk down the road and get a taxi off the street to take us to another hotel. Fortunately, this worked better and we did at last settle down to a panic free night's kip. In the morning at breakfast Stan said we had to get out of the country, but they would be watching the airport for us, so he would take our tickets to a travel agent to see if they could be changed for a ship sailing to England.

We were in luck: the TSS Masdam of the Holland American line was sailing that day to Amsterdam via Southampton and our tickets were exchanged for five first class berths to Southampton. We packed our cases, walked down the street and got a taxi to the port. Arriving at the port we saw the Massdam and it did look quite large, but the only other time I had been on a boat was from Southampton to Jersey and that was a ferry with the Boys Brigade so I had nothing to compare it with. As cruise ships went the Massdam was quite small, built in 1952 with a gross tonnage of 24,300, catering for 39 first class, 854 tourist class and a crew of 228. Being first class passengers we had priority boarding and were allowed to board ship before the economy passengers.

Once on the ship Stan told us to go to our cabins, stay there and not look out the portholes until we set sail. Our purser greeted us and escorted us to our cabins; he must've found it quite strange that four long-haired English lads were travelling first class with only weekend cases for an eight-day cruise. Our cabins were pleasant with en-suite bathrooms, but compared with today's cruise ships they would look extremely old-fashioned, with no air-conditioning just a large fan to circulate the air. However, the other facilities available made up for it: a large main lounge, promenade, veranda café, sun deck, sports deck, our own purser, breakfast in bed and à la carte dinner menu. Apart from our drinks everything was paid for so it was a matter of relaxing and enjoying a well-earned rest.

As I lay on my bed I relived the events of the past week, starting with our flight to America, being wined and dined, put up in an apartment by a record company, meeting one of America's most famous attorneys, being hunted all over New York to sign a recording contract and making our escape on a cruise ship. It's quite ironic that it was only five years earlier that I was an electrician sitting on the scaffolding of a new house in Hythe overlooking the Solent, eating sandwiches with my mate Brian Cowen as we watched cruise ships sail by, saying, "Wouldn't it be great to be on one of those?" and there I was, sailing out of New York as a first class passenger. I wonder if Brian ever got his cruise?

It seemed quite a while before I heard the sound of the ship's horn and then felt the swaying of the ship as we pulled away from the quay. It wasn't long before Stan was knocking on the door inviting us all down to the bar for a drink to celebrate our escape. After a few drinks we got talking to the steward and enquired about the other passengers on board. He told us the ship contained about 20 first class passengers and 800 American students going to Europe for their summer vacation, 500 girls and 300 boys. We couldn't believe our luck with hardly any old fogeys or screaming kids on board but a boatload of people our age looking to have a good time; we couldn't have asked for anything better, and were looking forward to what could be an interesting and hectic eight days.

Our first meal on board was dinner and we were required to wear jackets and smart shirts. We all had jackets and trousers but no ties. As it was the first dinner of the cruise it was not so formal but we realised that would have to get ties from the on-board shop to conform with the dining etiquette for the remainder of the cruise. The food was excellent, escargots, frogs' legs, steak, virtually anything you wanted and it was delicious. Our older first class companions were very curious about us and our appearance, but Stan was well spoken, very smart and a complete gentleman, so they soon accepted us and became very friendly.

Carl, who shared our table, was the typical American boy: short cropped blonde hair, well-built, suntanned and making us look like something out of The Hobbit. Poor Carl could not understand our humour especially when we started taking the mickey out of each other; he thought we were being serious. Even when we told him a joke he didn't get it, but this worked both ways: when he told us a joke, we would be waiting for the punchline only for him to say, "Didn't you get it?" then all together we would say, "No."

Although there was this barrier with humour we did get on very well with all our first class passengers and when they eventually found out who we were and why we were on board they were very intrigued. As word got around the ship about us we started to mingle more with the other passengers and it all became good fun as they wanted to know all about us.

As I mentioned there were 500 girls on the boat and the captain must have felt it was his duty to protect the privacy of the other first class passengers from any possible disturbances that could be caused by us taking girls back to our cabins. He decided to put a security guard on duty in the passage outside our cabins. It was quite ironic that they were keeping their eye on us, when down in the tourist class everybody was sleeping around and smoking marijuana. We decided we would have a bit of fun and pretend we had smuggled a girl to our cabin. The plan was, I would dress up as a woman and Carl would pretend to be raping me. So, in the lounge with the help of our female first class passengers I borrowed high heeled shoes, skirt, blouse and a big summer hat and two oranges from the restaurant for my tits. The ladies made a great job with putting on my makeup and when they had finished arranging the oranges, hat and skirt in the right positions I was ready. Stan looked at me and being gay went into convulsions, his face went bright red as he held on to a nearby column to stop himself from collapsing on the floor; I thought he was going to have a heart attack.

The plan was for me and Carl to walk past this very fat guard who was sitting on a stool in the passageway then go into my cabin and close the door and wait for the knock on the door. We did this and waited but nothing happened so I said, "We'd better cause a bit of commotion," and suggested I would make it look as though I was trying to escape and Carl would be dragging me back in the room. We opened the door and I told him to give me a little push and then jump out and drag me back in as I screamed. This he did, and again we waited, but still no knock at the door; perhaps they realised it was a hoax, but we decided to have one more attempt and I told Carl to push me really hard and again drag me back in. He certainly did push me hard, and I hit the wall hard the other side of the narrow passage. He then picked me up and dragged me back in to the room as I screamed in a falsetto: "You dirty yank!"

Again we waited for the knock, but there was nothing. I said, "Have a look down the passage." He opened the door, had a quick glance, then said, "Jesus Christ, there are about five officers at the end of the passageway." We were both elated that our prank had worked and decided to walk up to them and hope they would see the funny side of it. We opened the door and I pulled the big hat over my face and walked arm and arm towards the crew that turned out to be the captain, the ship's doctor, the fat security officer and one other. At that particular time I had a cold sore on my lip and just as we got right up to our welcoming committee I lifted my hat and said to the doctor, "Have you got anything for a cold sore?" I soon realised that the Dutch sense of humour was not compatible with ours, as not a single smile appeared on anybody's face, but I did then appreciate that Carl and I sometimes did have a compatible sense of humour as we both started laughing. The captain, still expressionless, muttered, "Very funny."

When the captain learnt that the whole of first class was in on this prank he did mellow and smiled when the other passengers mentioned it. As the captain often dined with the first class passengers we became very friendly with him and I was invited up to the wheelhouse and allowed to steer the ship for a while. When I say the wheelhouse in those days you did have a big wheel rather like those on galleons. (See photo).

The only other notable thing was the 4th of July, American Independence Day. When you consider that 800 of the passengers were American, we did feel a little bit vulnerable, so Stan told us to keep a very low profile just in case they got a little bit carried away with their celebrations. To our relief the day went off without any hostilities towards us.

When we eventually arrived in the Solent we started to say goodbye to our fellow passengers. Throughout the cruise we signed many autographs and made lots of friends and now it was time to say goodbye. Carl was particularly upset that we were going and it seemed like the whole ship had come to wave us off and many were wiping the tears from their eyes as we pulled away in our tender. The TSS Massdam was sold a year later on September 29, 1968 to the Polish Ocean Lines and was renamed Stefan Batory. Its final resting place was a scrapyard in Turkey in 2000. For us it was back to the reality of record contracts, managers and solicitors, all the things we had escaped from in New York.

Escaping New York on the Massdam

The captain lets me steer the ship

Reg tasting the culinary delights

Me and Carl on the Massdam

CHAPTER 19

On 26 June 1967 whilst we were in New York Larry served a writ against Harvey Block Associates and us, claiming damages and seeking an injunction to restrain us from looking for a new manager. A preliminary hearing was heard in the High Court in July and our counsel successfully argued against the injunction restraining us from engaging new managers. I will not bore you with the legal jargon as it was so complicated but to put it in layman's terms, Lord Justice Stamp said he could not grant the injunction because it would force us to work with Page when our trust and confidence in him had gone. This left us in the position of being able to negotiate for a new manager but not able to sign anything until we knew the outcome of an appeal Page One had lodged.

Meanwhile Chris and Stan were returning from the preliminary hearing to Reg's apartment in London where the rest of us were waiting to hear the verdict. This was quite a tense and important moment as we waited for the knock at the door. When it eventually came, Stan came bowling in with a big smile on his face and holding high two bottles of champagne saying, "We did it." We all jumped in the air as Stan popped the cork and we drank to our new beginning. Stan described the atmosphere in the court and the look of thunder on the faces of Hookum and Crookum as the verdict was given. Chris said he got most upset when their barrister tried to taint his character by saying that he lived in an apartment with his fancy woman. This he found completely unnecessary and it did show what depths they would sink to.

However, jubilation was short lived as we were then told that this was just the first stage and the next stage would be to win back our contracts.

At the hearing we unfortunately did not win back our recording contracts and had to fulfil our obligations under that agreement, which meant we had another two years tied to Page One Records. We also could not prove any misappropriation of our money. This we found very difficult to prove as Page One were our record company, managers, music publishers and agents so they had all the information we would require to prove any misuse. It would be quite ludicrous to think that Page One would supply us with any information that could incriminate them.

We did however win back our management and agency contracts and that left us free to look for a new manager and agent.

Because Stan put all the money and effort into the creation of the Troggs and getting us away from Page One, it was only fair that he and Lance should be rewarded and take over managing us on a bigger commission than their original 2½% each that Larry gave them. The next step was to get an agent, preferably one away from the London scene and all the wheelers and dealers.

Danny Betesh had a successful booking agency, Kennedy Street Enterprises, based in Manchester, and he represented Freddie and the Dreamers and Dave Berry and had promoted the first Beatles tour. From our point of view the most exciting prospect was that Danny had promoted tours in the USA for Freddie and the Dreamers, Hermans Hermits and Wayne Fontana: just the type of agent we were really looking for. So after a meeting Danny did agree that he would try to arrange a tour of the USA, something that Larry did not want us to do. (For what reason? Most probably he thought they could make more money out of us in this country.)

Prior to our adventure in America 'Night Of The Long Grass' was released and reached number 17 in the charts. This release was another turning point for us as it was the last time that Larry and Colin would commandeer the B-side.

Three of my concerns had been remedied: the management, the B-side issue and our bookings. We all felt that we were at last beginning to break away from the people that once had complete control over everything we earned and recorded. The only information that we didn't have direct access to was record sales and money received. It took Elton John with a court case against

Dick James Music in 1982 to reveal the scam that Dick James was doing. (I will talk about how we benefited from this later on.)

When Larry received our letter indicating our intention to cancel our contracts he released a recording from our album 'Hi Hi Hazel' - why he released this we don't know as it had already been released on the album and had no chance of doing us any good whatsoever and reached only number 47 in the charts.

As you can imagine with the court case and the release of this record, we were not very happy with Larry. We had to prove that we didn't need him and that we were able to do it on our own, but we needed a hit record to prove it.

I don't believe Reg was a religious person even though he was always looking up at the sky in the evening and saying, "I wonder if there's anything out there" - this was more about aliens than the spiritual world - but he did say that listening to the Salvation Army one evening on the television, singing about love being all around, gave him the inspiration for our next hit. When he finished the lyrics and tune we arranged a practice. With Reg singing, Chris playing the riff on a 12 string and Ronnie and me joining in with the drums and bass, we knew we had something special and thought it could be a potential hit. It was different from 'Wild Thing' and would prove to be just as popular. As it was Ronnie's turn to have the B-side we rehearsed one of his songs, 'When Will The Rains Come.'

The recording session was going to be quite strange as we normally had Larry there directing us, but due to the court case there were naturally a lot of bad feelings and it would take a little while before the wounds would heal and we would be able to work together again in a relaxed atmosphere. Fortunately, we had Colin Frechter our musical director who took charge of the session. We found this was more beneficial to us as he could count us in, conduct, and as Ronnie said, "sprinkle a bit of fairy dust" by adding any additional instruments that might be required. When Reg put his voice down and Chris did the harmony, everyone agreed that we could have our next hit. As we had previously rehearsed the numbers back in Andover it didn't take us long to get Ronnie's song down. We were very eager to hear the final mix of the two numbers but that would be done at a later date.

When we eventually got our copy we took it around to Stan's. He eagerly put it on his Dynatron radiogram, laid back on his very expensive settee, closed his eyes and listened. As we waited for his comments a big smile appeared on his face and he nodded saying, "It's good, it's got to be a hit."

'Love Is All Around' was released in November 1967 and peaked at number five. Hallelujah! We did it on our own without any input from Larry and this would confirm that we had the talent and we could do it without him. There must have been a feeling of déjà vu for Larry as he was in the same situation as in 1965 when, after a long court battle, he also lost The Kinks' management contract and they went on and had success without him.

Our new agent Danny Betesh arranged tours in Scotland and Ireland and television and concerts in Holland, and we also did the usual television shows here, like Top of the Pops, Dee Time, Ready Steady Go and Crackerjack. Top of the Pops was always something to look forward to, where you would meet top artists, watch them perform their latest hits and even get to talk to them in the canteen. Not all the artists were performing live: some were recorded on location elsewhere, or earlier in the week in the studio. I remember one time when Jimi Hendrix was on stage ready to perform his latest hit. As he waited somebody accidentally put on the backtrack of Alan Price and The Amazing Dancing Bear. Jimi stood there scratching his head and looking around bewildered then said, "I don't know the chords to this one man."

On 8 July 1966 we were sitting in the canteen of the 'Ready Steady Go' studios at Wembley having a break from filming a Walker Bros Special, when we noticed Simon and Garfunkel sitting opposite and decided to go over and introduce ourselves. They invited us to join them. The first thing Paul Simon said was, "It looks like you guys are going to stop me getting to number one in the States," as he had written 'Red Rubber Ball' that was recorded by Cyrkle and was at number three while 'Wild Thing' was number one. He went on to say he had written it for the Seekers but they had turned it down. Cyrkle were originally called the

127

Rondells and were managed by Brian Epstein. He went on to tell us the strange circumstances regarding his song 'I Am A Rock'. He released an album in 1965 on the CBS label, titled 'The Paul Simon Song Book' featuring the song 'I Am A Rock', and later on that year it was released as a single, but sold few copies. In 1966, he teamed up with his partner Art Garfunkel, who gave it a more commercial feel and then it shot up the American charts. CBS also released it on an EP called 'I Am A Rock' so it had been released four times i.e. album, single, EP and a single with Art. They were very interested in us and asked if we had been to the States yet. We said unfortunately not, but we hoped to get over there soon to cash in on 'Wild Thing'. He said the American scene now had changed from the sweet sounding songs of Bobby Vee to the heavier groups like the Beatles, Jefferson Airplane and The Who and that was the place to be. He added he thought we would go down a storm there; little did we know it would be another two years before we would be able make our way there.

Ready Steady Go studio

'Love Is All Around' was the pinnacle of a very turbulent year as we celebrated Christmas and toasted for a prosperous 1968. In

February we released another one of Reg's compositions 'Little Girl' and Chris supplied the B-side 'Maybe The Madman.' 'Little Girl' reached number 37 and that would be the last time we would enter the charts. In April we released another of Reg's songs 'Surprise Surprise' and I wrote the B-side 'Marbles And Some Gum.' I really liked 'Surprise Surprise' and had big hopes for it, but we were not able to get the television or radio cover and it became an uphill struggle.

The start of 68 was not looking good, with poor record sales. We began to realise that we could no longer rely on having extra income from that source, but would now have to make a living doing live shows.

CHAPTER 20

Being the only single member of the band I had other things on my mind, and when not gigging I would be spending time seeing Hilary and wondering if our future would be together. After we had broken up three years earlier I was very upset; knowing how upset she was about breaking up with Richard, we both must have decided that we might as well stay together. I know it's shameful to admit but she had to remind me how and when I proposed to her.

Apparently, after a Foresters New Year's Eve dance at the Fiesta Hall, we returned to my mother's house, went into the front room, stretched out the settee and I said, "If I asked you to marry me what would you say?" Her reply was, "If you ask, you'll find out." Maybe it was because I had had a few too many to drink and felt a bit romantic that I said it; I did love her and did want to marry her, but I laughed it off. I never asked again as we both must have assumed we were going to get married because we started looking for a house.

After inspecting several properties in Andover we decided on a three bedroomed detached house in Wolversdene Road with a third of an acre. It was a lovely looking house with white rendered walls and bay windows either side of the front door and a white flowering cherry tree in the front garden. It was a nice area and was situated on a hill overlooking the town. We thought we could happily live there and decided to buy it.

Our first home

Danny Betesh, our new agent, had for the last few months being trying to arrange a tour of America for us, and finally he reported to Stan that everything had been finalised and it would start in March. If we had any doubts about leaving Larry they had now dissipated as he would never let us go there. After reading Ray Davies's book and learning about the problems they had in America when Larry left them and came back to England, I realised that he must have thought that America was a taboo place for him. There was also his cock-up with 'Wild Thing' over there.

Things really started to get busy with the excitement of an American tour coming up, buying a house, arranging a mortgage and being asked to do a publicity stunt with Hilary. The story was that I had not officially asked her to marry me and it being a leap year she would wait no longer and would ask me. The photos and write-up made the nationals and was good publicity for the group, but Hilary gets quite annoyed when I tell people we only got engaged because of a publicity stunt which is not true. She never asked me and I never asked her, we just took it for granted we would get married, but she did remind me that I hadn't bought her a ring yet and I would need to buy one before I left for America which was the following day, so we rushed up to the Walworth Rd London, to a pawnbrokers.

You might think it was strange going to a pawnbrokers, but Hilary lived near there when she was a young girl and remembered walking past and looking in the pawnbroker's window and seeing all those amazing rings on display and dreaming one day she would have one. We arrived at 4.30, half an hour before the shop was due to close, and she couldn't make up her mind between two and kept picking up one, putting it down, picking up the next, putting it down. Not being flash but getting bored after she kept saying, "I don't know which one to have," I said, "Why don't you have both of them?" She eventually chose a sapphire with two diamonds, and that in her mind made it official. I thought I had shown my commitment when a few days earlier I left her a blank cheque to put down on Wolversdene Road knowing I'd be in America when the completion went through. I suppose it would have been nice if I had been a bit more romantic but things were so hectic it was just a matter of getting the things done.

We arrived at Kennedy airport two years after 'Wild Thing' was number one. The press seemed more curious rather than excited with us: the interest could have been far greater if we had arrived when 'Wild Thing' was number one, but that was all in the past now and we had to move on and prove that we were more than just a group that had hits with 'Wild Thing' and 'Love Is All Around.'

Touring in another country in the 60s did create certain problems. The biggest concern was always the equipment; if that failed, as we had found out in Sweden, and then you had to borrow. With poor equipment, or equipment that played up, you could spend the bulk of your time on stage twiddling knobs, flicking switches, changing leads and generally sorting out problems rather than entertaining the people who had paid to come and see you.

This could cause frustration, arguments and bad feelings in the group.

Fortunately we negotiated a deal with Baldwin Burns in London and were pleased that they could also supply us with all our equipment in America and would replace, or repair as necessary, through their dealers in America. The American Baldwin amplifiers were completely different from the ones we used in the UK. The Exterminator was massive, with a 250 Watt amp and 2x15, 2x12 and 2x7 inch speakers all built into one cabinet that stood five foot tall and was on roller castors so it was easy for the roadies to wheel them about.

As this tour was nearly 50 years ago I was unable to find any accurate references on the dates and places we played, but will tell you the most interesting and amusing stories that I remember.

In the late 60s drugs like marijuana were commonplace in most of the big cities in the USA. This came very apparent to us when we were booked for a gig in Greenwich Village.

When we arrived at the venue, which was a small dance hall with a stage and everything painted black, it had a strong smell, one that I was not familiar with. It reminded me of burning incense in a church. We were greeted by an African American man with dreadlocks who held out his hand to greet us saying "Hiya man." With a smile on my face I went to shake his hand, but he just slapped my palm; this took me completely by surprise. I had seen black people do this before but I thought it was just when a black man greets another black man. When I asked why he did it, he replied, "Don't wanna get no contamination man," then went on to ask me if I had any shit. I had no idea what he was talking about but soon realised that we had entered a world that was completely alien to us and began to feel concerned about how we would fit in, not having, or smoking, any drugs. Even more worrying: would they understand our music?

The evening started with a black man with no teeth sitting on a chair playing an acoustic guitar singing 'Helena Rigby.' His name was Richie Havens and he was a regular at this club. I can't remember their name but the other act there had more speakers on stage than The Who would have playing in a stadium; the strange thing was they were a folk group and could have got away with an amp and speaker each.

The most memorable part of the evening was the display projected on the backdrop behind the artists as they played. There was somebody holding a glass tray containing water with different coloured oils which was projected onto the backdrop, the movement of the tray from side to side making the globules look as though they were dancing to the music; then there was a film of an old train steaming by, followed by a penis and a film of Charlie Chaplin and his funny walk. This was all about heavy psychedelic drug effects and our only addiction was to our Rothmans.

When we took to the stage we didn't know what to expect. After the first couple of numbers we realised that the crowd sitting on the floor were not in this world but completely out of their heads and were more interested in looking at the strange effects on the backdrop behind us. Poor Reg tried everything to get some response as he pranced around the stage gritting his teeth and swinging his arms all over the place singing our hits, but it was like playing to a load of zombies with mouths and eyes wide open and blank expressions on their faces. Fortunately this type of gig was just a one-off.

The American way of life is completely different to ours, especially with the police and a large proportion of society carrying guns. I remember one event well, when our flight to Denver was delayed and we were concerned we would not get to our gig on time. The promoters were also worried and arranged a police escort for us from the airport to the venue; this made us feel very important having a police car with flashing lights and siren sounding, speeding in front of our taxi whilst jumping all the red traffic lights. This was great fun and we encouraged our driver to enjoy the experience and go faster; it must have looked strange for bystanders seeing a taxi chasing a police car rather than the other way around. We did eventually get to the gig on time and were very grateful to our police escort.

After the gig the police were still hanging around and we got chatting to them and invited them to a party in one of our rooms at the Holiday Inn. To our surprise, they said they would love to come. We arrived back at the hotel with police car, two policemen, some female fans and booze and we were ready to party. We were rather intrigued with their police guns and asked them if they could do any tricks. They proceeded to show us a few cowboy tricks, such as spinning the gun around their finger, then putting them back in the holster and drawing them again quickly. This was done to be friendly and impress, but left me feeling quite concerned as they didn't seem to appreciate the seriousness and danger of carrying these weapons, especially after a few drinks when they took their holsters and guns off and threw them on the bed and started dancing. For me a good party was ruined, as I was forever keeping my eye on the guns laying on the bed, thinking it would just take one nutcase to cause mayhem in this room. My mind went back to a year earlier when we were in a nightclub in Paris and some idiot got out a gun and started firing it into the ceiling causing us all to dive under the table.

After Denver we made our way to the southern states of Mississippi, Alabama etc. Whilst there on 4th April the news came in that Martin Luther King Jr had been assassinated. This caused an instant reaction of anger among the black people and set off riots, and a curfew was imposed in the town we were due to play, and the gig was cancelled. I don't know if there had ever been a curfew in England, definitely not in Andover, although in 1830 three hundred farmworkers broke into Taskers the agricultural machinery maker and started to break up machines in their workshops, especially the threshing machines that were thought to be robbing them of their work, until a large force of police were called in to quell the mob.

Getting bored after a day's travel and just sitting around the hotel, we thought we would go into town, but after seeing all those armoured vehicles and soldiers speeding up and down the road and being told by the hotel management that a curfew meant if we were caught wandering around the National Guard would shoot us, we decided to have a night in and watch the TV.

We were quite pleased to move on down to Miami and sit on the beach. It felt somewhat safer after Mississippi, even though we did feel a bit like misfits sitting on the beach, skinny, white with long hair and looking like aliens as we watched the bronzed bodybuilders with surfboards walking by, accompanied by bronzed bikini clad young girls. After a while I think curiosity got the better of them and somebody came over and asked who we were. When we told them they couldn't believe it and these four aliens soon became the centre of attention and were invited to a beach barbecue that evening; it turned out to be great evening, with dancing, music, drinks, food and a lot of autograph signing.

The next morning was so lovely that after breakfast Reg and I decided to go on a sea fishing trip. We made our way down to the quay and hired a man, boat and fishing tackle. Whilst we were at sea Reg thought he would try and get a little bit of a tan and stripped off to his shorts, not realising the strength of the sun and not heeding the warnings from the boat man. It wasn't too long before his body was quite red. About four hours and three small fish later we returned to the harbour. Getting off the boat for Reg was quite a painful exercise as any movement of his legs against his trousers caused him discomfort. His first stop on terra firma was to find a chemist for treatment. He did look quite comical as he came out of the chemist with his arms full of painkillers, creams and sprays and walked stiff legged to the car. At one point we were concerned that he would not be able to do the gig that night, but after a tepid shower, painkillers, creams and a lie down he managed to get through the evening albeit not in his usual energetic way.

Reg and I enjoying a morning fishing in Miami before he got sunburnt!

When we arrived in Texas we all thought it would be a good idea to ride the range and be cowboys for a day. This might sound strange when you consider our experience with the polo ponies a year earlier, but since then Stan had got friendly with John Darcy, an Irish horse dealer, who lived just outside Andover in an area with open fields, marshland and woods where you could learn to ride. When I had time off I often went there and eventually lost my fear of riding and enjoyed galloping (well, maybe trotting) through the woods. One evening I was talking to Keith Moon in the Cromwellian Club in the Bayswater Road and he told me he was very depressed and hated his lifestyle in London. I suggested that it might do him some good if he visited Andover and took a horse out and, maybe, switched off; he thought this was a great idea. I gave him Stan's telephone number and told him I would mention to Stan that he might contact him. While doing the research for this book I was told by Alan Grindley that Keith Moon and his girlfriend did stay at Stan's and I heard the story that one morning Keith came down the stairs at White Cottage holding a glass of brandy, tripped and fell from top to bottom, but never spilt a drop out of his glass. Waste not want not.

Our first riding lesson at Shepards Spring

We did have a lovely day on a family ranch with the father and his young daughter really showing us what proper riding was when they pretended to round up cattle, but we were quite happy just to jog along and tell people that we had been riding the range in Texas.

Riding the Range in Texas

Whilst in Texas we also decided we must go to an Indian reservation. With many tribes originating from that state it was not difficult to find one that catered for the tourists. Walking around the teepees and totem poles chatting to the Indians we found it interesting but it soon became apparent that they were just as interested in us as we were in them. Two young Indian boys came up to us and asked us for a souvenir, preferably from Carnaby Street, but not having anything other than the clothes we stood up in were unable to oblige. Rather than disappoint them I told them if they came to my hotel in the morning I'd give them a souvenir but they would have to reciprocate by bringing something Indian.

The next morning at 7:30am there was a knock at my bedroom door. Still half asleep I staggered to the door, and opening it I found the two Indians standing there, one holding a miniature lacrosse bat. Standing there in my pants I invited them in, and then rummaging through my suitcase I found two psychedelic neckties

139

from Carnaby Street. I handed them over, and their faces beamed as they stared at the psychedelic patterns and bright colours; they then handed me the miniature lacrosse bat. To my amazement one of the Indians started to wrap the tie around his forehead and tie it in a knot, but his friend quickly removed it and told him it went round his neck. Turning to me, he smiled and said thank you, and then they both left.

Because of the distance between gigs travel was usually by air or road; most of the time it was by road. On one occasion we passed a restaurant displaying a sign stating that all their staff were topless. Our eyes nearly popped out our heads and we screamed to our roadie to pull over. We swung into the car park and no sooner had Alex parked the car than we were out like greyhounds from their traps and on our way to the restaurant entrance. Entering the dining room we eagerly looked around for the bare bosoms, but soon realised that we had been duped, as all the staff were male.

3rd-4th May 1968. Ronnie and I sharing our birthday cake. Holiday Inn America

Our American tour was coming to an end with San Francisco and Disneyland California our last two gigs before returning home.

140

The tour had been very successful and plans were being made for a second tour in two months which would incorporate Canada. After getting confirmation of our flights Reg and Ronnie contacted their wives and asked them to let Hilary and Toots (Chris's girlfriend) know of our arrival time. We landed at Heathrow and passed through customs, and as we entered the arrival hall I saw Pat, Brenda and Toots as they came flying past me and threw their arms around their loved ones' necks; I stood there wondering where Hilary was. I felt a little embarrassed and awkward when they asked me where she was, adding they'd told her of our arrival time; to this I had no answer but would telephone and find out. As this was before mobile phones, the only means of communication was the public telephone boxes at the airport which had long queues, so rather than keep the others waiting I decided to wait until I got home.

CHAPTER 21

It was quite strange getting back home to see the family again but Mum and Dad had some bad news. Shirley's schizophrenia had got so bad that she had been sectioned and had been taken away in an ambulance to a mental hospital in Basingstoke. I felt so sorry for them as they must have had a really rough time as they described her loud and violent mood swings. I decided I would take Mum over to visit her straight away.

Park Prewitt was a very big Victorian mental health hospital built in 1921 which had served as a military hospital in the war until 1946 when it reverted back to a mental hospital containing fifteen wards. Walking through the main reception we met all sorts of people, some talking to themselves and some just staring. We made our way down the corridor to Shirley's ward. When entering we couldn't believe our eyes: we saw Shirley on all fours under a table howling like a wolf. We both found this very distressing and stood there in disbelief. We were then approached by a nurse who enquired who we were, and who we wanted to see; still in a state of shock we muttered one word "Shirley." The nurse went over to the table and helped Shirley up telling her that her mother and her brother were there to see her.

As the three of us sat down on the battered old armchairs, Mum gave Shirley some biscuits and fruit, then put a comforting arm around her shoulders. This act of compassion was abruptly stopped when my mother said, "Where's all that water coming from?" and turning round she found a male patient, with a smile on his face, pissing all over her and soaking her handbag. She was horrified and jumped up yelling, "You disgusting creature put that away!"

A male nurse came hurrying over saying, "He hasn't finished yet," before guiding the perpetrator away. As you can imagine this scene took on a humorous flavour which was never appreciated by my mother, who was always 'keeping up appearances'. What had started out as a depressing day with Shirley in the depths of despair was lifted: this single act really made her laugh so much, together with our mother's 'Mrs Bouquet' mannerisms, that it lifted Shirley's spirits more than any of her NHS drugs could have done.

Unfortunately, for all of Mum's good intentions she ended up more distressed than Shirley, especially as we were driving home on a hot day and no amount of lavender water splashed over her could completely hide that distinctive smell. While still in Park Prewitt Shirley met Alistair, another patient, who she married and then lived in a flat in Basingstoke with until he died in 1996.

Getting home from the hospital I realised I hadn't contacted Hilary yet to say I was safely back and find out why she was not at the airport to meet me. I was thinking perhaps she couldn't get the time off from work or was unable to get transport. I was surprised when I found the real reason. Apparently, all the time I was away I never contacted her once, and her father was just as annoyed as she was as he had spent all his spare time painting the outside of our new house and it seem that I didn't care. He must have thought that I was just playing around and not really serious about my future commitments to his daughter. This was far from the truth as I've always loved Hilary and getting married and spending our lives together was my dream. Unfortunately because of the hectic life I was living I was not always thoughtful in my actions, or more accurately inactions, but the one thing I was sure of was my sincerity. I arranged to meet her over at the house the next day and then apologised, but made the point that when I was travelling things were very hectic and sometimes it was very difficult to find the time to ring home, especially with the time differences. As much as I wanted to have a rest at home I did say I would take her away on holiday to make up for not being more considerate while in America.

Hilary and I, 1968 at Mum's house

We had a lovely week in Cornwall and on returning decided to get started with the painting. Hilary chose the paint and I started the next day. Duck egg blue was chosen for the stairs, landing and the hall, with white gloss for the woodwork, and it didn't take me long to get the emulsion on the walls and ceiling. Living with Mum and Dad I never got the chance to do any painting so when it came to the undercoat and gloss I found this a lot more difficult as you just can't slap that on. Finding it boring I started to rush to get it finished. Unfortunately while I was holding the paint can in my hand and dipping the brush in, some paint ran down between my fingers causing the can to slip out my hand, and to my horror I watched it merrily bounce all the way down the stairs splashing the walls as it went. I couldn't believe it: I just slumped down on the top stair with my head between my knees nearly in tears wondering why the professional painters on the building sites never got into such a terrible mess. I then decided from that moment that I would do the job properly and purchased brand-new brushes, rollers, sandpaper, overalls, paint kettles and dust sheets. After cleaning up my mess I set off in my new frame of mind: take your time, work tidily and don't rush. Following those few simple rules the job was soon done stress free and, I will say, very acceptably.

In July we released 'You Can Cry If You Want' penned by Reg and the B-side 'There's Something About You' by Ronnie. 'You Can Cry If You Want' was a lovely song, but there again, not what the record buying public wanted. Meanwhile Danny Betesh and Premier Artists had been working hard for our second American tour. It would start on 16th July and finish 14th August with the possibility of more gigs to follow. It would start in Ottawa and end in Cornwall New York and gross $38,000. We would also be playing a few gigs in Canada with The Who and record a Coca-Cola advert in New York. If we had any doubts about leaving Larry they had now dissipated as he would never allow us to go to the States.

Our second American tour and doing gigs with The Who was great fun. Keith Moon, like Ronnie, was volatile and at times unpredictable, but he was very likeable and told us stories how he kept explosive charges that he would put in the door jambs of hotel doors and blow them off their hinges. His mischief didn't stop at hotels as Ronnie found out to his expense. Ronnie was a very heavy drummer and usually had a minimum of six spare sticks attached to his kit. One night while laying into his drums he couldn't believe it as every time he picked one up and hit the drum, he ended up with half a stick in his hand; it was not until the end of the gig, after examining the sticks that he found that the bulk of them had been sawn halfway through. Ronnie knew straightaway who the culprit was: his mate and fellow drummer Keith.

Although Ronnie had on this occasion had defective equipment, albeit sabotaged, my sympathy was with The Who's roadie.

Every night after Pete Townsend had smashed up his speakers and guitar and Keith had kicked his drums over. The poor roadie looked very much like Mr McHenry of the Magic Roundabout with a bald patch on the top of his head and long black hair hanging down to his shoulders. I'd watched him painfully hobbling around the stage, as he suffered with gout, picking up the remains of the equipment that were wrecked in the evening's performance.

Wondering what he was going to do with it all, I curiously enquired "Do you have replace all that damaged equipment?" "No," he replied, "I have to repair it." Then he had to transport it to the next gig for it to be smashed up again, the poor bugger.

Being on tour is not the healthiest of lifestyles mentally or physically, especially being cooped up in a car for the best part of the day with everybody smoking, coupled with late nights and drinking. There are times when your body will remind you it deserves a little more consideration and as most of our meals in America and Canada were in cafes which did not serve vegetables, just salads, I did feel at times that we must be deficient in vitamins and we would often watch our American road manager, Loren Schwartz, swallowing handfuls of vitamin tablets as though they were Smarties.

Not only were vitamin pills very popular with Loren, he also liked to smoke a joint and it was not uncommon for him to be smoking whilst driving us. This didn't seem to affect his driving ability or speech, but sometimes I wondered if he knew he was driving a car, or what he thought he was driving. Strangely, we seemed to be more concerned with breathing in the smoke trapped in the vehicle, as we would wind down the windows and frantically wave the smoke out.

None of us really took up drugs and I was always concerned that, as I couldn't give up cigarettes, I'd have no chance if I got hooked on them as well, but Reg and Ronnie did briefly try marijuana. Reg said that after a joint, when he went into the shower he could feel every drop of water hitting his head. Hippies, peace, love and marijuana portray a picture of friendly dancing happy people, but when Ronnie took marijuana it made him aggressive and all he wanted to do was to fight everybody. I'm glad he never got hooked on marijuana otherwise a happy hippie camp could have turned into a battlefield.

WILD THING

DATE	CITY	TOTAL FEE	VIA I.M.C.	VIA PREM T.	VIA TROGGS
16th July	Ottowa	₤2000.00	- - - - -	1000.00	1000.00
17th "	Montreal	2250.00	- - - - -	1035.00	1025.00
19th "	Halifax	3000.00	- - - - -	1500.00	1500.00 *
20th "	Virginia Bach	2000.00	- - - - -	1000.00	1000.00
23rd "	Richmond	2000.00	- - - - -	- - - -	- - - - **
24th "	Philledelphia	2000.00	- - - - -	1000.00	1000.00
25th "	Jackson	2500.00	- - - - -	1250.00	1250.00
26th "	Montgomery	2250.00	- - - - -	1125.00	1125.00
27th "	Birmingham	2250.00	- - - - -	1125.00	1125.00
31st "	Whitchita Flls.	2000.00	- - - - -	1000.00	500.00 ***
2nd-3rd August	Oklahoma	3000.00	- - - - -	1500.00	1500.00
4th Aug.	Hidden Valley	2380.00	- - - -	- - - -	2380.00
5th "	Denver	344.09	344.09	- - - -	- - - -
8th "	Sudbury	2000.00	- - - - -	1000.00	1078.00
9th "	S.St. Marie	2000.00	- - - - -	- - - -	2143.00 ****
10th "	Fort William	2000.00	- - - -	1000.00	13.00 ****
12th "	Cornwall	2250.00	- - - -	1035.00	1250.00
?	?	Record Commerc.	1500.00	1500.00	- - - -	- - - -
		₤37724.09	1844.09	14570.00	17889.00

Fees collected:

Via I.M.C.	1844.09
Via Premier Tal.	14570.00
Via Troggs	17889.00
	₤34303.09

** Total fee due from The Who — 2000.00 }
*** Cheque as yet uncleared — 500.00 } - If all these fees are
**** 50% deposit not yet } received that are outstand-
    received from S.St.M. — 1000.00 } ing, then the total monies
                            3500.00 } for this tour would realise:-
                                                    34303.09
                                    Plus o/s fees   3500.00
                                                    ₤37803.09

(This means that the Troggs will receive approximately 80 dollars
more than the total contracted fee for the tour ..... this is
probably the change left over from the currency changes etc.
between Canada and the United States).

* 19th July Halifax fee received was ₤1500.00 by Troggs less ₤300 Tax
but for accounting purposes gross fee is shown.

US Tour schedule

147

One night in Canada I felt a bit tired and went to bed early. As I was lying there relaxing, my whole body suddenly started to shake uncontrollably. This really frightened me as in the past, when things have been really hectic, I had experienced weird whizzing Catherine wheel noises in my head, but this uncontrollable shaking was something completely different. Not knowing how to stop it I tried mind over matter and completely relaxing my body, but all to no avail. Eventually, to my relief, it gradually stopped. I knew the next day I would have to see a doctor and tell the others my condition, just in case I cracked up and couldn't complete the tour.

Next morning I knew I had to tell them but decided to wait until after I'd ordered breakfast. Sitting there very quietly as the others chatted away I wondered what their reaction would be. The waiter eventually came to take our order and said, "Morning lads, did you feel the tremors last night?" The complete sense of relief I felt was similar to your doctor advising you that your test results were clear, and from having no desire for food my appetite certainly returned as I ate a full breakfast. I can't remember in what part of Canada this happened but apparently earth tremors were not an uncommon event. I only wish I'd known that before I went to bed.

On 12th August we did our last gig in Cornwall New York. After recording an advert for Coca-Cola we were ready for our trip home, but before we were able to leave the country we had to submit accounts and pay the taxes on the money we had earned.

The day before we were due to leave, Alex and Jonah informed us that they would like to stay behind in America for a holiday before returning. As we had no work lined up for a week we agreed, but we never saw them again. Apparently, Alex married a girl who worked for Premier Talent and Jonah tried his hand at being a pop star. At that time in the States there was a big interest in British artists, mainly due to what the Americans called the British Invasion, where the Beatles, Stones, Kinks and Who were more popular than the American artists. Jonah was able to secure a record contract with Decca and released a record purely on the fact that he was English and could sing a little bit. His record was not a success and he soon got disenchanted with all the wheeling and dealing associated with the industry; he gave it up and became a carpenter and settled down in Canada.

It was good to get back home to see Hilary and look at the house. But there was not a lot of time to relax as we were then told that Alex and Jonah would not be coming back and we had to find another driver and roadie.

Hal Carter was born in 1939 on Merseyside and moved to London to work for Larry Parnes; he then became the road manager to Marty Wilde, Billy Fury and The Kinks. As he had previously worked for The Kinks and was now looking for work Larry suggested that he would be a good replacement for Alex. We all agreed and with the addition of Steve Beanie, our new roadie, to drive the van and look after our equipment, we were ready to start gigging again.

It was a very special occasion for us on 29th August when Billy Fury played at the Guildhall in Portsmouth and we were his support act. Hal was in his element as he was originally Billy's road manager and they were also very good friends, so much so that on arriving at the Guildhall Hal said "Would you like to meet our Bill?" For us it was a great privilege meeting one of the early rock stars who we had listened to on jukeboxes in our youth. As we walked into Billy's dressing room he was standing at a table sticking stamps into a big album. He was quiet but very friendly. After describing some of his favourite stamps, his life in Liverpool and his friendship with Hal, we said how good it was to speak to him and then returned to our dressing room to get ready for the first half of the show. The Gamblers, a six piece combo, opened the show, followed by Alan Field the compere. Then there were The Slade Brothers, a duo from Canada, and we then finished off the first half. Being a local band we certainly got a fabulous reception. The second half was opened by Alan Field followed by The Peddlers, a jazz trio, then it was Billy's turn, and we all congregated in the wings to watch his performance. I looked across at Hal as Billy was singing 'Halfway to Paradise'... he had a great big smile on his face and a look of real pride.

Hal was a typical Scouser and had a funny squint in one eye - I think you call it a lazy eye - that seemed suddenly be looking

149

somewhere else. I remember sitting next to him travelling at high speed down the M1 late one night; when I looked across at him and noticed his eye was closed, I couldn't believe it - I thought he was fast asleep! Leaning over but not wanting to scare him or make him jump I softly said, "Hal, are you awake?" He slowly turned to me and said, "Of course I am." More in relief than in anger I said, "Well, your bloody eyes were closed." He then explained that when driving he would rest one eye at a time and unfortunately the eye nearest me was the one that he was resting.

Still hoping that we had not lost our ability to produce a hit record we were again disappointed when 'Hip Hip Hooray' in September 1968 failed to impress the record buying public. With our last four records not making the charts a certain amount of despondency started to creep into the group. Without a hit record many of the promoters would not risk booking us, but with working the Northern cabaret circuit and gigs on the continent you could make a living. However, without the record royalties we were all very aware, in the words of Bob Dylan, "The times they are a changing". The most worrying situation was being told by our accountant that our previous accountant had never submitted any accounts to the Inland Revenue and that we had to be prepared for a very large tax bill. This was quite a frightening prospect but it could have been worse if I had not heeded Stan's warning to put something by for tax; he had suggested that I regularly purchase Tax Reserve Certificates. These could be bought from the bank and could only be used to pay your tax; the other advantage was you earned interest on them, albeit very low. Over the year I purchased £1000 worth of the certificates but later found out they would fall well short of the amount I would need to cover my tax bill.

CHAPTER 22

1969 did not start any better with the release of 'Evil Woman' again generating little interest and no income. Page One must have also been feeling the pinch as we were their main act and were not generating any decent sales for them. This prompted them to do what I believe was a very selfish and stupid thing, getting Ronnie and Reg to record solo records and Chris his own LP. This, in my view, was the start of the end for The Troggs.

The first problem occurred when we were booked to do a television show for Southern Television. We arrived at the studio ready for the rehearsal, but Chris hadn't arrived; we rang his flat but there was no answer, so we assumed he was on his way and carried on using a stand-in. Much to our disappointment Chris never made it and we ended up using the stand-in for the live show. When we contacted him the next day to find out why he hadn't made it, he said he had worked until the early hours of the morning on his LP and overslept. It seemed to me that everybody now was out for their own ends and any consideration for the others was non-existent. I did ask Chris what would happen if his records made the charts, what would he do about the band, and he replied, "We'll cross that bridge when we get there."

After the failure of Reg and Ronnie's solo releases Page One rereleased 'Wild Thing' again. I've heard of companies re-releasing records that never quite made it which later became hits, but not re-releasing a record that was already a massive hit, considering people would already have the single, EP or LP anyway. Needless to say this did not make any impact on the charts.

Although not very busy we were doing a few gigs, mainly in Sweden and Germany; but my mind was on my future wedding on 6th April.

In between gigs I helped where possible with the arrangements. Hilary arranged the bridesmaids' dresses, flowers, invitations and the catering and I arranged the transport, venue, band and the hiring of the morning suits from Moss Bros. I also had to notify the police that with it being market day and with the possibility of fans turning up, there could problems for traffic on the road at the entrance to the church.

It was a sunny but very windy day as I walked up the steps to the church, noticed the previous bride's veil flapping around in a tree and prayed that wouldn't happen to Hilary. After our vows we made our way back past the congregation to a small room at the front of the church, where we signed the register to the sound of 'I vow to thee my country' echoing around. After signing the register we made our way outside, and as the church bells rang we were greeted by family, friends, fans, the press and confetti. The day was going so well, until I accidentally trod on Hilary's train as we exited the church causing her to stop dead, turn and give me a dirty look. It was the only glitch in a wonderful day. After the reception at the White Hart Hotel we went back to Wolversdene Road to change into our going away outfits. Steve Beanie, our road manager, then took us to our hotel in Luton, where the next morning we caught our flight to our honeymoon destination, Majorca.

Hilary's parents, us, and my parents

All together: Ronnie, Hilary's sister-in-law June, Gerald Staples, Reg and Chris. Small bridesmaids Sarah and Jane

Signing the register

After a week in Majorca we returned to Wolversdene Road a married couple, looking forward to our new life together. We pushed open the front door, which was held back by the accumulation of flyers and sales circulars you always get when a place is left empty. I started sifting through the pile and throwing away all the rubbish only leaving the brown and handwritten envelopes. Gradually working my way through the utility bills that were not too depressing, I then opened one from the Inland Revenue - a belated wedding gift, a tax demand for £7000. Today this would not seem a lot of money, but when you consider the house that we had just bought cost £6,800 you can appreciate that it would now represent a considerable amount of money. When Hilary told her father about our tax demand he said, "I think you've married the national debt." I knew I would have to pay the tax, and with my Tax Reserve Certificates and a year of austerity I gradually managed to clear this debt. Because I had saved Tax Reserve Certificates, the Inland Revenue agreed a payment plan that allowed us to keep the house. Hilary was the only one that had a regular job and weekly wage working at Norton Villiers, the motorcycle company, so her wages were taken each week as part of the payment plan. This was not a very good start to our married life, but what was to follow a month later I have always found very difficult to understand, and to come to terms with.

Meanwhile we had our regular tour of the Swedish Folk Parks and the odd clubs, but while I was away Hilary had to go into hospital to have an operation so I was pleased when the tour was over and I could get back home to see how she was.

CHAPTER 23

On 15th May, Reg rang and said Larry wanted to see us in his office that day, but could offer no more information. Our drive to London seemed no different from any other time apart from wondering what Larry had to say. After parking the car we made our way to Page One's offices in Oxford Street, where we were greeted by Larry's receptionist informing us we could go straight in as Larry was waiting for us. As we entered the room he was sitting at his desk alongside a very official looking man. He asked us to sit down and introduced the other person as Page One's solicitor, then turning to me he said, "Pete, the boys don't want you in the group anymore." I couldn't believe what he was saying and it left me completely speechless.

I was even more confused when Ronnie said it was because my taste in music was different from the rest of the band. Then to completely confuse me, Larry equated it to a football team, saying, "When they are not winning they have to make changes." Chris said nothing, but Reg came out with the big stab in the back and said in a very nasty way, "And if you don't go, I won't sing anymore." What an arsehole, after all the years we had worked together, recording his songs and making him a fortune, he for no apparent reason came out with such a vicious remark. I couldn't believe that a month ago they were all celebrating at my wedding, eating and drinking and sending me a good luck telegram.

Larry had two contracts already written up and ready for me to sign; this was to release them from any further commitment regarding the management and recordings, and in return I would receive two months' wages from Troggs Limited, this amounting to £200, the B-side of the next release and an undertaking that I would still be entitled to any future royalties on records I had already played on. Needless to say I would not sign their contract until I had taken some legal advice. It was then suggested that we should see Mr Stark, our accountant, and inform him of the situation. Before I left the office Larry advised me: "Don't go telling the press because it will look bad for you."

After leaving Page One, we made our way to Gray's Inn Square and Mr Stark's office. We were invited in and Reg informed him that I was no longer a member of the group. A look of utter amazement came over his face, and turning to me he said, "What's your game then?" Again, I felt as though I had done something wrong, but for the life of me I couldn't think what. It wasn't until Mr Stark mentioned The Troggs' debts and the amount of money we owed his company, that I realised he thought that I was trying to opt out of any liability regarding that money. After hearing it was not of my choice, he became more understanding and told me that he would be in touch regarding The Troggs and my accounts. With that we left his office. Reg, Ronnie and Chris went their way, and I mine. It would be another 13 years before we would ever talk to each other again, and even then it turned out to be a very acrimonious meeting.

I took a taxi to Waterloo and caught the next train back to Andover all the time wondering what Hilary would say, but I was very surprised that after telling her she didn't seem unduly worried. With the dreaded tax bill still hanging over us, I'm sure deep down she must have been very concerned, but didn't let it show. Personally the thing I found most difficult to handle was trying to explain to people why I had left the group. It wasn't until fairly recently I could tell the truth and say, "They kicked me out," rather than "I just got married and didn't want to travel anymore."

The first two weeks at our new home were a bit strange, but since it was summer there were many things to do in the garden and around the house and, being newlyweds, we were learning to live together, unlike today when you live together then get married.

I did call around to see Stan who was just as amazed as I was when I told him what had happened. He asked me what I was going to do, but my head was completely blank of any ideas. He then went on to mention a friend of his, Jack Winkworth, who had had a good joinery/cabinetmaking business until his wife left him and he lost all interest and motivation. He suggested that it might be a good idea if I bought the business and contracted Jack to work for me for the minimum of two years. This would give me an income and Jack a living without any worry. Within a week we had signed a contract, and from Jack's small double garage we had Andover Woodworking up and running. Our workshop was Jack's double garage which was fitted out with all the woodworking machinery; the only extra thing I had to buy was a van.

Because Jack had been depressed and had lost motivation, I acquired his backlog of unrepaired antique chairs, tables and cabinets to repair and eventually return them to their owners.

Jack was a fantastic cabinetmaker and was highly respected by all the antique dealers and wealthy people around the area. Unfortunately, woodwork was never my forte so I was very eager to do whatever I could to make myself useful including making the tea, sweeping up, making deliveries and doing the office work. We were both happy in our work which helped us to get over our recent dramas. Although I loved doing the antiques, purpose-made windows, doors and staircases became the major part of our work. There came a point when the two of us could not cope with the workload and needed to take on extra staff and a larger building. I found a small factory unit just outside Andover that would serve our purpose. After installing the electrics I employed five more people for the workshop and we were soon up and running.

Jack's wife was Italian with relations in Naples and he invited Hilary and me to travel down to Naples in his car and stay with them. As we had never been to Italy we thought it would be a good idea. Andover to Naples was a long drive but apart from losing the sump plug and oil it was quite an uneventful but beautiful journey. The most memorable part of the holiday was when in Naples I hired a small rowing boat. With Jack and Hilary sitting in the back I rowed to this lovely cove, but because it was so choppy I couldn't get right in to land the boat. Jack decided to jump in and help pull the boat ashore, but as he jumped in he didn't realise that he was so short and the water was so deep and he disappeared completely under the boat. I anxiously looked over the side hoping that he

157

would reappear, when suddenly a hand came out of the water followed by a bald head with a big lump of toupee dangling from it. Jack looked quite comical attempting to hold his toupee in place to regain his dignity at the same time as trying to drag the boat ashore.

In the past I've learnt that when things are going well that's the time I should worry, and this was the case when Jack found a new lady friend, who seemed to take up most of his time even when he should have been at work. Jobs were left unfinished and quotes were not done. I eventually tackled Jack about the situation and he said if I wasn't happy he would go.

In 1974 the miners went on strike causing rumours of coal shortages that could affect power stations with the possibility of power cuts. My problem with Jack, my right hand man, coupled with the thought of my workers being unable to use the machines, made me decide to sell the business and move on. Fortunately I managed to sell quickly, just before the start of the power cuts and the three-day working week.

Four years on from leaving The Troggs, I was again back in the same situation, wondering what I was going to do. Throughout that four year period, Mr Stark, the group's accountant, kept me informed of the group's activities when he called in to see me on his way to Southampton to do an annual audit. I learnt that the person that replaced me, Tony Murray, who played in another one of Larry Page's groups Vanity Fair, had been used to do some bass work on our album 'Mixed Bag' while I was away on my honeymoon. From that point my fate must have been sealed. Mr Stark told me they employed him on a weekly wage, but had to reverse that arrangement when later they found he was earning more money than they were. I was also quite surprised when he told me in 1972 that Chris had left the group and had gone to Portugal to run a cafe/bar. He was replaced by Richard Moore, a guitarist from Canada. In four years the group had lost two of their original members and with that their unique sound.

CHAPTER 24

Hilary and I decided to do a pub management course with a view to having our own country pub. We applied to Ind Coope and after letting our house we were sent to Hemel Hempstead to train in a pub. Our living accommodation was in the attic and very cramped and it didn't take me long to realise that perhaps this wasn't going to be our future. Hilary wouldn't come down to the bar in the evening because of all the smoke and the customers talking about all their problems. Our training seemed to consist mainly of carrying a drunk landlord up the stairs in the evening and dumping him on his bed. If that wasn't bad enough Hilary discovered she was pregnant; I say bad enough, but in actual fact I was quite pleased, even though the timing was not good.

On our days off we just wanted to get away from that dump, so we would stay with Hilary's mum and dad. On one of our days off, Hilary discovered red spots all over her body and decided to get it looked at by her doctor. After examining her he asked, "Where have you been?" Quite puzzled she said, "Why?" He replied, "You've been bitten by fleas." This caused a problem as we would now have to tell our hosts their pub had fleas.

We did not expect the angry reaction we got from the landlord, when Hilary told him she had been bitten by fleas. Even though he had a big dog he insisted that we must have brought them into the pub and told us to pack our bags and go. It didn't take long for us to throw our clothes into suitcases and make a quick exit out the door, thankfully on our way back to Hilary's mum's.

Because of our never-ending tax burden, the first thing Hilary did when getting back to her mother's was contact an employment agency to get work. The next day she was lucky enough to get an interview and was told she could start the following day.

That evening in bed she started to have stomach pains that continued through the night. In the morning I contacted the doctor who suggested that I take her straight to A&E at Basingstoke Hospital. Arriving at the hospital she was put in a wheelchair and wheeled away. I sat in the waiting room praying everything was going to be okay. Eventually a nurse came into the room followed by Hilary and said, "I'm sorry but your wife has lost the baby."

With all the recent upheavals I don't think I took all it in and it wasn't until we were walking back to the car she said she had a D&C.

Arriving at her mother's I was a little concerned how she was going to take the sad news, but was surprised when she said, "Well you will just have to get on with it, and put it behind you." With that Hilary said, "Right I've got to go to work, can you drop me off?" I couldn't believe their lack of emotion at such a traumatic time, but knowing how embarrassing Hilary would have found it displaying her emotions and getting sympathy, I know she would just keep it inside. Her mother, Mary, who was brought up in a very poor area of London where large families and infant deaths were commonplace must have found it sad, but this was something she would have experienced many times before. Like me I'm sure there have been times, when alone, they both have shed a tear.

With Hilary working and me finding electrical work things felt less pressurised. We also had some good news: the man renting our house in Wolversdene Road was being relocated with his job and had to move up north so he asked if he could terminate his rental agreement with us. Although Mary and Len looked after us well we just wanted to get back to our own house.

In 1976, three years after we left Len and Mary's, Hilary became pregnant again. The summer of 1976 was one of the hottest and driest summers on record with clear skies and nine weeks of temperatures reaching 30°, not the sort of weather to be carrying a baby. We both became quite concerned when on her weekly visit to the doctor he told her the baby was not putting on enough weight and advised her to rest more. She told him this was not possible as she was still working. "You must give up work and rest more or you could lose this baby," was his firm reply. The thought of losing another child was such a frightening prospect that when she got home the first thing she did was to ring her boss informing him that she would not be returning.

When Hilary went into labour I was advised to take her to Winchester Hospital and on 1st September between the screams, tightly gripping my hand, and shouting "Don't you ever bloody do this to me again" she gave birth to a little girl we named Lydia. After holding my daughter and seeing Hilary was all right, and being told that all she wanted was rest, I decided the best place for me to be would be down the pub. As I walked across the car park I was surprised to see a flash of lightning, followed by the loud rumble of thunder and the glorious feeling of rain on my face. What an unbelievable day: I became a dad and the nine week drought ended.

My mum and dad with Lydia

The following year I heard the sad news that Stan Phillips our manager had lung cancer and was not expected to live. I rang his house and the phone was answered by a male nurse. After explaining who I was, I asked if it was possible for me to visit him; he said yes but explained that Stan spent a lot of time sleeping due to the powerful drugs he was on. Arriving at White Cottage, my mind drifted back to the 60s as I could recall all the parties and sex that had taken place in the cottage. After knocking on the door I was invited in by the male nurse. Stan was lying on a bed in the lounge with his eyes closed. I approached him and said, "Hi Stan, it's Pete." He tried to open his eyes but couldn't, but smiled; unfortunately because the amount of drugs he was on he was unable to speak.

Our manager. Stan, in America with us

I stayed another ten minutes and thought this is probably the last I'll see of this man, the one that did so much for The Troggs and for me, even after my exit from the group. I cannot speak for the other members of the group but personally I owe Stan Phillips and Lance Barrett a big debt of gratitude for their initial input into our early careers, for without them, there would have been no Troggs.

Later the sad news came that Stan had passed away and the service would be held at St Michael's All Saints, Weyhill. Looking around the congregation, which included of a large party of his Welsh relations, I could see Brenda, Reg's wife, and Lance, but nobody else I knew. Stan was laid to rest in the adjacent graveyard. A while later I revisited his grave which by now had a headstone, with the inscription 'He did it his way.'

Hilary's mother had severe angina and in 1978 we decided to move to Basingstoke to be nearer and help out if needed. Being a self-employed electrician I could go anywhere. We found a lovely new development in Old Basing, a village just outside Basingstoke. Wolversdene Road was a very desirable area and it was not long before our house was sold to a local doctor and we moved in to our new house in Rainbow Close.

In 1982 I was working as a contracts manager for an electrical company in Basingstoke, when I had a call from the Andover police telling me that they had some bad news and that my father had been found dead on the pavement in London Road. They were with my mother who was in a very distraught state. I told my boss the situation then went straight to Andover to comfort her.

After my brother identified Dad's body we proceeded with the funeral arrangements. The funeral was held at Salisbury crematorium. It was quite unfortunate but I'm sure my dad would have seen the funny side of it: it wasn't until we were leaving the crematorium that my mum said, "Didn't you realise that today was also your father's birthday?" ('The Lord giveth and the Lord taketh' - in my dad's case on the same date). Our family have always had coincidences with dates, as the next year would highlight. Following a thunderstorm, again, Hilary gave birth to our son Leo in Basingstoke hospital. Not only were both our children born in thunderstorms they were both born on a Wednesday on the first of the month and following a bank holiday. Leo was born on the 1st of the 6th month, Lydia was born on the 1st of the 9th and our telephone number at the time was 61019: is that creepy or is that creepy?

I had not heard from Mr Stark for a while, and therefore I never knew what was happening in The Troggs but heard, via the grapevine, that Chris had returned from Portugal and rejoined Reg and Ronnie. Tony Murray, who replaced me, had left the group and his replacement was Peter Lucas who at the time was playing with Dozy, Beaky, Mick and Titch.

I was surprised one day when The Troggs' new manager contacted me asking my permission to use my likeness on promoting the group. Not wanting to be forgotten as an original member I agreed but I was surprised to find on a advertising poster they used my body and Peter Lucas' head. I did find it quite sad that they were trying to remove my very existence from The Troggs. Even in the online Troggs fan club article, The Story of The Troggs, my name was not mentioned once.

In 1985 Elton John won a High Court battle with Dick James about the misappropriation of royalties. Listening to the outcome on the TV, I wondered if he had done the same thing to us. So I was not really surprised when after 17 years Reg contacted me and said he had been in touch with Elton John's solicitor and had told him Dick James had also been our record company and music publisher and it was possible that he may not have paid us all the royalties we were due. He agreed to act for us but he also needed me to agree. Seeing the large settlement Elton John got, I was eager for them to press ahead as soon as possible so I gave my consent. We had one meeting with the solicitor then left him to get on with it.

After many months of negotiating with Dick James' solicitors a full and final settlement of £70,000 was agreed. But before we actually received the payment we heard that Dick James, whilst playing cards at home, had collapsed and died. It would take another year due to the complications caused by his death to get the money. Eventually Reg rang me from the solicitor's office and informed me that they had received the money, then handed the phone to the solicitor to explain the situation. He told me that their fees would be £11,000, Reg would get £43,000 and the rest of us just under £5,000. And I had a personal bill of £2,888. I was amazed how much Reg was getting and suggested he could contribute a bit more to the solicitor's bill; I heard him mumble my suggestion to Reg, then he came back and said Reg was not prepared to pay any more. That old familiar feeling of frustration returned that I had experienced years before with that unashamed grabbing and lack of consideration for others. I was pleased not to be living in that environment.

If I felt something was unfair, I was unable to keep quiet. This of course would make me look like a troublemaker, and I can see why Reg would want to get rid of me.

That would be the last time I would ever speak to Reg, as in 2013, most probably linked to his heavy smoking, he died of cancer. Although I did feel very sorry for Reggie's wife Brenda and her family, I just could not go to his funeral. I would have found it very difficult to have the appropriate sentiments for that sad occasion.

In the 80s I did hear that Ronnie had a drink problem and was eventually asked to leave the group and was replaced by Dave Maggs.

Ronnie was great fun but was prone to get himself into some hilarious situations. If you have listened to 'The Troggs Tapes' with Reg and Ronnie in the recording studio and the continual use of the F word you would appreciate that the F word was a major part Ronnie's vocabulary. One time in Sweden a young pretty female reporter asked him: "What is this word 'fucking' you keep saying?" Ronnie was quite taken aback, because he didn't know he was saying it half the time. With Reg and Ronnie swearing so much you might find it hard to believe that in all the time I have known Chris, I have never once heard him swear. When researching this book, I did ask one of his ex-girlfriends if she ever heard him swear and she said, "His favourite swear word was sod it."

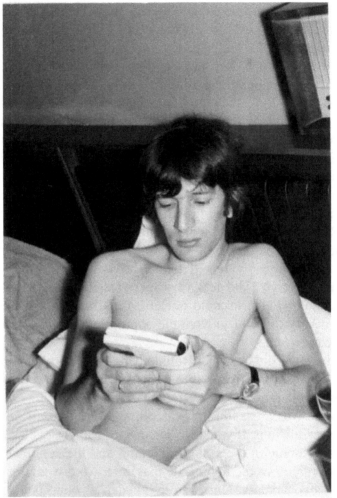

Ronnie, a great guy who died far too soon (13.11.1992) is reading one of
his favourite Mickey Spillane books in Manzis Leicester Square 1967

We played a lot in Sweden, especially The Folk Parks. I
remember on one occasion after a gig as we drove away, six lovely
blonde girls were waving us goodbye and shouting, "Wankie,
Wankie." We couldn't believe what we were hearing and asked our
driver to stop. As the young girls came running over we asked them
what they were shouting, and they repeated, "Wankie Wankie."
We asked them why they were saying that and they replied that the

Mersey Beats had shouted it as they were driving away last week! We did impress on them that those words were for men only and not young ladies. They looked very embarrassed and said sorry, and as we drove away we shouted "Bye!" and they reciprocated.

CHAPTER 25

After coming out of the group I wanted nothing more to do with music, but in 1994 I had a call from John Walker telling me that he had just bought a set of drums and would like to re-form the Ten Feet Five but purely as a get-together to have a bit of fun. None of us were really keen to relive our youth but John was such a clever manipulator that it wasn't long before he had found Malcolm Porter (Charlie) the lead guitarist, I had bought a new bass and amp and Chris Penfound, after only planning to buy a harmonica, ended up buying a Fender amp and Strat. We had our first practice at Chris's house, which was great fun, and we decided to hire a hall the following week so we could turn the volume up. After many weeks, with the addition of more equipment, we decided to do a gig. What started off as a bit of fun gradually grew until we were doing quite a few gigs.

The gig I remember most was at Docklands in London. John's wife worked for the Prudential insurance company and they were having their Christmas party on a barge that had been converted into a Chinese restaurant with a separate dance area at the other end. On arriving we set up our gear, while at the other end of the barge the staff were enjoying their Chinese meal and the usual company speeches.

We felt a little uneasy, as when we'd finished our first set the party was still going on at the other end of the barge and no-one seemed to know we were there; even though they were paying us and giving us Chinese food. We thought that in the second half, the partygoers would be well tanked up and let their hair down and join us. However, through the second half no-one came over and we were beginning to wonder if we were in the wrong place or had got the wrong date. As we finished our last number the party at the other end of the barge finished and the staff gradually left; one person on his way out enquired if there had been a party here at our end. When we told him that we were booked for the Prudential party, he said, "Nobody told us you were here."

We had some marvellous fun but such is the life playing in a group, with family commitments and work, it sometimes becomes a bind and the band packed up.

Ten Feet Five 1996 Me Chris Penfound, Dave Smith, Charlie Porter and John Walker seated

I left the Ten Feet Five and started my own group, which I named The Wild Things that included my son Leo on rhythm guitar, Leon Munkley drums, John Fletcher lead guitar, Andy Kennedy saxophone and Opkar Hanns on keyboard; he also could play lead and drums. Being a 60s group we did mostly parties and corporate functions. Leo has always been fascinated by gadgets and when I purchased a smoke machine he was in his element playing with it. One evening, at a very posh hotel, whilst we were on stage he left the machine on too long and we were all consumed

169

in the smoke. While I was still trying to locate the members of the group through the smoke the fire alarm was activated and everybody had to evacuate the building. Switching off our instruments we made our way outside with the staff and guests, some of them in their dressing gowns. In the distance we could hear the sound of approaching fire engines and see their red flashing lights as they sped up the drive towards the hotel. Jumping out of their engines the firemen raced into reception, but it wasn't long before the scare was over and they climbed back into their engines and let us return. They told us it was a false alarm. We all laughed amongst ourselves saying it was more than likely Leo and his smoke machine, but I don't know if that type of smoke could set off the alarm. I did take his toy away for the rest of the evening.

The other booking I vividly remember, but the one I would most like to forget, was playing at Hilary's works annual party. This was another expensive hotel where a sit-down meal with wine and accommodation was provided for us. I didn't sit with the rest of the group at dinner but sat at the top table with the boss of the company. Halfway through my meal I noticed Leon pointing to our lead guitarist sitting next to him. I couldn't work out what he was trying to say until later he told me John had drunk two bottles of wine. I was a bit concerned, but I have heard that some guitarists need a good drink before they can play and I hoped this could be the case with John.

This would prove to be wishful thinking. When we started our first number, John was playing something completely different. After battling through two songs with John falling all over the place, the alcohol really kicked in and he fell backwards collapsing on Leon's drums, causing Leon to shout, "Get him off the fucking stage." We bundled him off the stage and continued the rest of the evening without a lead guitarist; fortunately Andy, a very talented saxophonist, saved the day by doing all the solos. By the end of the evening he had blown so much, his lips were in a permanent pucker position, looking like an orangutang's arse. After we got rid of John we were lucky enough to get Moon who was a guitar tutor. When Leon left, Peter Jenkins took his place. Eventually, as so often happens, the group gradually disbanded. Apart from John, I was very privileged to be in a band with some really talented musicians, and even today I am pleased to say they are great friends.

The Wild Things Leo, me Pete Jenkins (drums), Moon and Obkar

171

The Wild Things father and son

CHAPTER 26

On 3 October 2005 my sister Shirley died. She was Mum's second child to die before her. About a week before her death I took my mother to visit her in hospital. This went well, but I can't remember what we talked about. I do remember, however, that as we left her ward, Mum turned and waved goodbye and stood there staring for quite a while, perhaps knowing this could be the last time she would see her daughter. I did visit Shirley one more time on my own and that was the night before she died.

After Shirley's funeral Mum became very depressed and it was difficult for me to keep her company, go to work and also sort out Shirley's affairs. Dealing with Shirley's estate and Mum's depression began to have an effect on my health. Late one evening, about a month after Shirley died, I had a call from Mum saying an ambulance had arrived and was taking her to Winchester hospital for some tests. I was not too concerned as it was not unusual for my mum, when not feeling very well, to ring for an ambulance, go to hospital and get checked out; I would pick her up the next morning. However, when I enquired the next day how she was they told me that in the night she had had a stroke. I went to visit her and she really did look miserable and upset as she tried to speak but the words came out all wrong. With the loss of Shirley, coupled with not being able to speak properly, my mother gave up the will to live and stopped eating. Early in the year we had booked a cruise with some friends, but seeing my mother's condition I thought I might have two cancel it. I explained my predicament to her doctor and he told me I could do no more to help my mother and that I would need my health and strength in the weeks to come. Because I was feeling quite ill with headaches and dyspepsia I reluctantly took his advice.

When we returned Mother was still alive but only just. I held her hand and said, "Hi Mum, it's me, Pete." Her eyes opened a fraction then closed again. As I was leaving the nurse came up to me and said, "Do you want us to call you if it happens in the night?" I said, "No, leave it until the morning." I couldn't handle driving home on a moonlit night after seeing my mother die. I did get the expected call about 9 o'clock the next morning confirming that my mother had passed away in the night. Within nine weeks I had lost my sister and my mother, with two properties full of furniture and clothes to sort out; the doctor was right, I would need my health and strength.

In 2014 I was 70 and my wife told me my daughter was arranging something special for me but she didn't know what. In the meantime she would take me out for a special dinner. It would be at the Wheatsheaf in Dummer. As we made our way through a rather congested dining area that contained quite a few children roaming around I wondered where we would find a nice quiet spot to sit and enjoy my special meal. A staff member approached us and said, "Perhaps you would prefer it in here?" and pointed to a door.

On entering I saw loads of faces I knew: there was my next-door neighbour, my cousins, Chris Penfound from the Ten Feet Five, Leon and Opkar from The Wild Things and it wasn't until my grandchildren came running up saying happy birthday Grampy, and my daughter said happy birthday Dad and kissed my cheek, that I realised I was not dreaming and it was really happening. My quiet evening and special meal with my wife turned out to be a marvellous party with fifty friends and family enjoying food and drinks whilst being entertained by my good friends Alan and Chrisie Brill. Halfway through the evening they were joined by Leon, Opkar, Andy Kennedy and my son Leo, and I was invited on the stage to do 'Wild Thing' with my daughter, Lydia, playing the tambourine.

I finished with the number I did in The Troggs, 'Mona'. After my speech thanking everybody for coming and making my evening so special, I then called my half-brother Keith to join me on the stage for photographs. Since Mother's death I have regularly

174

gone out to dinner with Keith and his family. I think she would be very pleased that we have kept in contact, especially as I remember the last time Keith and I sat at her bedside in hospital she took Keith's hand and put it on the bed, then took my hand and put it on the top of Keith's.

Celebrating at my 70th with Keith

In 2005 Alan Grindley decided to make a film, 'The Story of Wild Thing.' Chip Taylor was touring in the UK and was performing at the Lantern Theatre in Romsey. Alan decided as he was in the country it was a good opportunity to film an interview with him, Chris and myself. After getting everybody's agreement we all turned up at his hotel the Potters Heron. I think I was the only Trogg that had never met Chip so it was very special day for me. I enquired with the receptionist if Chip Taylor was about and she said he was resting, but she would ring him and tell him I was there. I sat waiting in the reception area wondering what he would be like. When he arrived we shook hands, sat down and talked about 'Wild Thing' and our families. He was quietly spoken and

175

very pleasant and told me that he was playing in Romsey that evening and suggested I come and watch the show. I told him I would and thought perhaps Chris would be there as well.

My surprise 70th birthday party Alan Brill, Lydia, Christine Brill, Leon Munkley, Keith, me, Leo, Obkar Hanns and Andy Kennedy

That evening I went to the theatre and Chris was also there. Seeing us together Chip said, "Why don't you come up and play 'Wild Thing' with me?" He enquired with the sound engineer if there was a bass and another electric guitar in the building; since it was a music school it wasn't long before both were produced. This was a historical moment that would never be repeated. After sorting out the key we then ran through 'Wild Thing' and 'Any Way That You Want Me'.

That evening during his performance Chip invited Chris and myself to join him on stage where we played 'Wild Thing' and 'Any Way That You Want Me' together. What a unique occasion it was, made even more special as Brenda, Reggie's wife and Pat, Ronnie's wife were both in the audience, maybe reliving those earlier happier days. Another poignant fact of that evening was that Peter Davenport, one of my officers in the Boys' Brigade, who had witnessed my very first appearance playing my guitar in a trio at Moore Hall in 1958, was also there that night to watch what I was determined would be my last public appearance playing on stage. Yes, Wild Thing. (My rocky road.)

Chip and me

A treasured photo Chris Britton, John Platania (Chips backing guitarist), me and Chip

My family: mw, Lydia, Leo and Hilary

Gingers Addendum

Although we were doing well we didn't seem to be getting anywhere so we had to start thinking about writing our own songs which of course isn't very easy. I already had a bit of a tune rattling around in my head and eventually put some words to it, the song itself wasn't brilliant but at the same time it wasn't that bad, I needed to try and record it on a Grundig 4 track tape recorder we had by plugging two mics into a Watkins copycats using one mic for a 12 string guitar and the other mic for the vocals. When I played it back I was quite surprised as it didn't sound too bad, I played it to the rest of the boys to see what they thought of it and at first they didn't believe it was me.

Reg was quite impressed with what I'd done and said he also had a song he'd been working on so I got him to sing it to me so I that I could work out the guitar chords and we then recorded that as well. Both songs were on the slow side and not really our style but at least we had something to let people hear. So armed with our trusty Grundig, Reg and I went up to London again but this time we didn't know exactly who to approach, after a lot of thought we decided to go back to Lou Davis and ask the guys in the shop if they had any ideas. The guy who sold us most of our music gear said he knew a music publisher just around the corner in Denmark street his name was Pat Sherlock, go and see him and tell him I sent you. So around the corner we went and soon found Denmark Music Publishers, we went the upstairs and saw the receptionist and asked if we could see Mr Sherlock, after explaining who we were and who sent us she buzzed him on the intercom and then said to us ok, he will see you now and you can go straight in.

We nervously walked into his office and found him sat there behind a big desk, we sat down and explained who we were and what we were trying to do and he agreed to listen to our recordings, he sat there with no expression whatsoever on his face and we thought it wouldn't be long before he threw us out of his office, but to our surprise he said the two songs we wrote and recorded weren't that bad and then advised us to go home and record the whole group in a proper recording studio only this time he said record two of the best cover songs you do and try and write two more up-tempo songs of your own then come back and see me. We shock hands and thanked him very much for seeing us and also for his advice.

When Reg and I got home we told Dave and Ronnie and then went down to the Copper Kettle to tell Stan, his reaction was, great! Leave everything to me he said I'll sort it all out. The four of us soon got together and worked out the two best cover songs we would do but writing two more songs of our own was going to be a lot more difficult, it was Dave that came up with the best ideas for the two songs we had to do so we started to work on them as fast as we could.

In the meantime Stan had only gone and booked up a recording studio in Southampton without telling us and that meant we had hardly any time to write and practice the two new songs we were working on and if that wasn't bad enough he'd only booked us for a one hour session at 11am on the following Sunday morning. We left quite early for Southampton that Sunday morning just in case we had problems finding the studio but we didn't and so we got there with forty-five minutes to spare, this was good thing for us because it gave us a chance to calm a down bit. None of us had ever been in a recording studio before which of course made us all very nervous and we didn't know quite what to expect.

About ten minutes to eleven we started unloading the van and just after that the studio doors opened and two guys came out and said come-on the clocks running let's get your gear in and get it setup. After we got setup we had a quick sound check and then were told to start our first song which was "You Really Got Me" by the Kinks, after we finished the engineer said I'll play it back to you to see what you think. When we first listened to the playback we didn't think it was us because it sounded really great. You never get to really hear yourself when you're playing at a gig so this was actually the first time we'd ever heard ourselves properly and I have to say it was quite a pleasant surprise. We soon got started on our second song which was "Tell Me" by the Rolling Stones this meant I had to change to a 12 string guitar. This was also played back to us by the engineer and again it sounded great. The next thing we had to do was the two songs we'd written but this was more difficult due to lack of practice and the songs not being that good, we had two or three goes at both songs before they sounded a bit reasonable. We were really pleased with the two cover recordings we'd recorded but disappointed with the other two songs, but that was Stan's fault for being too eager booking the studio.

On the following Monday morning we phoned up Pat Sherlock and told him that we had taken his advice and been to a proper recording studio, he then gave us an appointment to come to London and see him only this time all four of us went. It was really exciting for us as it seemed at last we were getting somewhere. When we got to Denmark Music Publishers we went straight up the stairs and were told by the receptionist, the doors open you're to go right in, Mr Sherlock is expecting you. We walked straight into his office and introduced Dave and Ronnie to Mr Sherlock, we sat down and began playing our tape to him and again he sat there with no expression on his face and never said a word not until he got halfway through the fourth song when he suddenly turned the tape down and picked up his phone, we didn't know who he was calling but we hoped it wasn't the police. The conversation went something like this, *"Hi Larry its Pat Sherlock) – (listen I've got a group here I think you should hear) – (well I would if I was you because they do your boys record better than your boys do it) – (ok I'll send them around straight away"*.

When Pat put the phone down he said to us that was Larry Page I was taking too, he's a record producer and also manages a few groups the Kinks being one of them, he wants to listen to your tapes, his office is only a couple of doors away so you're to go straight round to see him. Well we all looked at each other and nearly fell off our chairs. We all shook hands with Pat and thanked him once again for all his kind help and then left his office to go and find Larry Page Productions which actually was only a couple doors from where we were. We went through the front door and up the stairs to the reception, when we got there Larry Page was just coming out of his office, he said hello boys go in and I'll be with you in a minute.

Shortly after he came back to his office he asked us our names and then said, you must have really impressed Pat for him to phone me up to so I'm quite prepared to listen to your tape, he then said he wanted to hear our tape played through his own recording system to hear exactly what we sounded like which, in fact we sounded ten time better than we did on our old Grundig.

After listening to our tape Larry seemed quite impressed and said if we were interested he would be prepared to take us on and manage and record us, we then had to tell him that we already had a manager to which he replied, don't worry about it I'm sure we can come to an arrangement, let me have his name and phone number and I'll give him a call. Larry then gave us a demo record and told us to go home and see what we could do with it and when we're ready he would have us back to record it at Regent Sound which was a studio just across the road which he used.

When we got back to Andover we went to see Stan who apparently knew all about it as Larry had already phoned him. We soon came up with our own version of the demo Larry gave us and it wasn't long before we were up at Regent Sound to do the recording. The studio was in a basement opposite Larry's office and I can remember it being a rather dark and impressive place with a great atmosphere, in actual fact it was the same studio that used by the Rolling Stones to record their first LP. After we'd finished in the studio we took our recording back to Larry who after listening to it said, yeah it's ok but not really good enough and then gave us another demo to have a go at.

It was about this time that I felt things were starting to go wrong; unbeknown to us Stan had made some sort of a deal with Larry and hadn't told us, we'd already signed a contract with Stan and now it seemed to me that Larry was taking over which meant as far as I could see we would have two managers. The thought of this started playing on my mind and what made it worse for me was things weren't going well at home either. My wife Jacqui was getting fed-up with me being out all the time and to be honest I didn't really blame her, but there again it was just the same for Reg and Ronnie's wives.

I also noticed that the group started arguing a bit more than usual which seemed to always leave a tense and an uneasy atmosphere. I wondered what the boys would think of it if we had to pay Stan 20%, Larry 20%, booking agents fees 10% and travel expense's another 10% because this would mean we'd only get 10% each of all we earned. I actually explained this to the other three but whether it sunk in or not I couldn't say, it seemed to me that fame was more important to them than fortune. As time went on the pressure of everything really got to me and I started wishing I'd never got involved with starting the group in the first place.

It all came to a head one day when Stan presented us with a contract to sign from Larry Page which I immediately refused to do; I told Stan that I would rather leave the group than sign it, this didn't go down well with Stan or the boy's and an argument soon broke out between us but I was adamant and I wasn't going to change my mind. While all this was going on Jacqui and I received a letter from Basildon Corporation Housing office offering us a second generation house which now put even more pressure on me to leave the group. After much thought and feeling totally fed-up with all that was going on I finally decided to leave the group and except this offer to move to Basildon.

When Stan realised I wouldn't change my mind and that I was defiantly going to leave he came to my flat to see me, the first thing he said was, you're very selfish doing this, which in some respect I suppose he was right but I was thinking more of my family than anything else. Stan then said to me, you know you're still under our original five year contract don't you which means any money you earn musically you'll have to pay 80% of it split between the and Troggs and myself, his threat made me see red and I stood up and told him that it wouldn't be a problem because 80% of fuck all equals fuck all. He then told me that the boys couldn't get another guitarist with the expensive gear that I had so would I be prepared to leave it behind to help the group out and he would carry on paying the payments. By this time I had really had enough and if by doing what he asked it would help the boys and at the same time get him off my back then I'd do it, but my opinion of Stan Phillips changed completely and I will never forgive him for selling us out.

We moved to Basildon shortly after all this happened but at first I found it really hard to adjust to the way things were although I eventually soon got a job and settled down. I thought I could now forget about Stan Phillips and the Troggs until one day a couple of months after we moved I received a telegram asking me to phone Ronnie at 7pm that evening. Ronnie had always been a good friend of mine and I was curious to find out what he wanted so at seven that evening I rang the number I was given and to my surprise it was answered by Stan Phillips who immediately said to me, don't hang-up Ronnie wants to talk to you.

When I spoke to Ronnie he said that Larry Page has given them a demo that was a dead cert for a number one hit and would I come back to play in the group, he told me I wouldn't have to move back to Andover as they could get round that, I told Ronnie that I couldn't give him an answer straight away I'd have to talk to my wife first, he said ok phone me tomorrow night at the same time and let me know. After hearing the names Stan Phillips and Larry Page mentioned on the phone I knew exactly what my answer was going to be and that was a definite no because I just didn't trust either of them.

I phoned Ronnie the following evening and gave him my answer; he then asked me why not so I told him straight, I just don't trust Stan or Larry anymore. This left me wondering why they hadn't got a new guitarist to take my place yet and several years later I did find out when I finally met up with Ronnie in Andover. Ronnie told me that every time they auditioned a new guitarist Dave Wright would keep telling them they weren't playing the songs the same way as Ginger did and understandably being told this it didn't go down that well with them. The last guitarist they auditioned told Dave if you want it played the way Ginger did I suggest you go and get him back, a short time after the auditions had finished Dave Wright left the Troggs as well. I'm not too sure what happened next but I believe our rival group the Ten Feet Five were either splitting up or had already split up and guitarist Chris Britten and Bass player Pete Staples must have got together with Ronnie and Reg to carry on playing under the name The Troggs. I can't be certain about this but maybe the dead cert hit Ronnie phoned me about was Wild Thing which five or six weeks after his phone call got to number one.

Acknowledgements

The year that it's taken to write this book has been quite hard and, at times, rather lonely, but I've been lucky to be encouraged and helped by the following contributors:

The Andover Advertiser
Mrs Jean Wardell-Davis on behalf of
Mr C E Wardell
Howard Mansfield (Ginger)
The Press Association
Colin Fretchter
The Middlesborough Gazette
Rex Features
David Gibson
John Walker
Chris Penfound
Bruce Turner
Arthur Smart
Tony Taylor
Chris Britton
Mr Trevor Photography
Wild Things 50 Ltd
Carmen Simon
Chip Taylor
Marianne Winkler

And special thanks to Teddie of New Have Publishing, Sarah Healey for her editing, Sarah-Anne for her valued introduction and my wife for a year's patience.

Lightning Source UK Ltd.
Milton Keynes UK
UKHW021056250822
407777UK00009B/1751